WRITE TO THE TOP

"Complain. If You don't, who will?"
—Paul Hawken
Growing A Business

How to Complain
& Get Results—FAST!

George Beahm

THE
DONNING COMPANY
PUBLISHERS
NORFOLK/VIRGINIA BEACH

To the Three Amigos:
Rusty, David, and Valerie

Edited by Robert S. Friedman
Cover design by Patrick Smith

Manufactured in the United States of America

9 8 7 6 5 4 3 2 1

First Edition

LIBRARY OF CONGRESS
Library of Congress Cataloging-in-Publication Data

Beahm, George W.
    Write to the top: how to complain and get results—fast!/by George W. Beahm; edited by Robert S. Friedman.—1st ed.
    p.   cm.
    Includes index.
    ISBN 0-89865-551-X (pkb.): $5.95
    1. Consumer complaints.   2. Letter-writing.   I. Title
HF5415.5.B43 1988
381'.33—dc19   88-14950
                                                                      CIP

Printed in the United States of America

Attention Schools and Businesses:

Donning Books are available at quantity discounts with bulk purchase for educational, business, or sales promotional use. For information write to: Special Sales Department, The Donning Company/Publishers, 5659 Virginia Beach Boulevard, Norfolk, VA 23502.

Table of Contents

Acknowledgments

I would like to thank my wife Mary, who always reminds me that some deadlines are more important than others, and my book editor, Robert Friedman, who applied the final twist of the wrench to tighten up the manuscript.

Introduction

There's a great short story by horror writer Dennis Etchison in which the convenience store clerks of California are replaced by zombies …and no one notices. Sheer fantasy? Consider this:

One day a friend of mine rushed into a 7-11 store to grab a six-pack of Coke™ sale-priced at $1.57. He was surprised when his cash register total came out to $3.75. Dumbstruck, he gazed at his purchase and saw that his six-pack was missing a can, so the clerk, without saying a thing, had rung up five single cans at 75¢ each! Yes, he had encountered the dreaded Convenience Store Zombie—he was living the horror!

When it comes to the problem of lousy service in America, convenience stores are only the tip of the iceberg. Respectfully submitted for your approval is the case of my former bank, Wells Fargo in Hollywood. This was undoubtedly the worst bank I've ever done business with. Opening a checking account was a major ordeal requiring the presence of three people and tying up my opening deposit—a cashier's check from Bank of America—for five days. Then they refused to give me a credit card for the electronic teller because, so they said, there were two signers on the account. (Other banks seem able to cope with this situation.)

After the account was up and running, I learned that making a simple deposit was a twenty-to-thirty minute chore, most of that time spent standing in line. The tellers were wonderful—all three of them, servicing a line of customers that resembled a scene from *Exodus*. When I complained about this to an "account executive," he shrugged and suggested that I use the automatic teller, which of course I could not do because they wouldn't issue me a card. I ended up using the night depository a few times, in the middle of the afternoon, but then had to track down someone to validate my parking ticket, which they didn't like to do because the night depository didn't spit out a receipt to prove that I'd conducted business there. And so it went for about a year, until I switched banks.

When *Time* magazine, in its February 2, 1987 issue, asked the ques-

5

tion, "Why Is Service So Bad?" and mentioned Wells Fargo Bank by name, I clipped the article and mailed it to the bank president. He did not write back. I should, of course, have written a letter of complaint detailing my problem and requesting a specific solution. But the only action that would have satisfied me (i.e., the swift execution of all upper level Wells Fargo executives) wasn't likely to happen.

Letters *can* be effective, though, if your wants are more reasonable.

For instance, in my college days my friends and I often found ourselves needing breakfast at three in the morning, so we became regular patrons of various local Denny's restaurants. I always ordered a particular one-egg breakfast combination and an extra egg. Sometimes I was charged a modest 30¢ for the extra egg; other times I was charged twice that for the egg as a "side order." No amount of arguing with a graveyard-shift manager could get the price lowered once it was established at the higher level.

That sort of thing annoys me. A foolish consistency may be the hobgoblin of little minds, but we're talking *money* here. So I wrote to the corporate offices of Denny's and stated my problem clearly and concisely, just as George Beahm advises you to do in this book, and for my efforts was rewarded with a beautiful letter on Denny's letterhead stating unequivocally that an extra egg served under the conditions I described should cost 30¢ and not a penny more. I placed this letter in my wallet and used it frequently throughout my college career.

But what about the *real* bucks? Forget 30¢ here and there—can mere letter-writing pay off when there's a *sizeable* sum at stake? The answer is an emphatic "YES!"

When I moved from a small suburb of Los Angeles into the heart of Hollywood, I dutifully informed my insurance agent of the move. My six-month auto policy with The Hartford of Connecticut was up for renewal at that time, so I renewed for $246.30. My agent did not tell me that my rates would more than triple as soon as The Hartford learned of my move.

Five months into this six-month policy I received a letter from The Hartford telling me that my premium had been adjusted and that I owed an *additional* $621.74 on the policy I'd bought for $246.30! I wrote back. I was calm but adamant: I would not pay this retroactive, unforewarned increase. By the time I heard from them again the policy had lapsed and I was insured by another company.

I will spare you the details. But what happened next was that I received and wrote letters. The Hartford demanded the retroactive premium; they referred my account to their collection agency (Dun and Bradstreet). I informed Dun and Bradstreet that the bill they were trying to collect was under dispute, and I wrote to The Hartford assuring them that I would not pay the extra premium. In all, I wrote four letters. Eventually we reached a compromise. I paid The Hartford $103.62 for the single month that I retained their insurance after receiving notice of the rate increase. That's a savings of $518.12—more than $129 per letter—and in retrospect I think I probably caved in too early. Another good letter might have gotten me off the hook completely.

You may think that writing letters is too much trouble to go to. Think again. These days you simply cannot afford to pay every bill that someone may decide to send to you. Sending out a bill is cheap and companies know that most people can be easily intimidated. People see themselves as standing alone against a vast army of collection agents, lawyers, and "account managers." You may be tempted to pay even when you don't think you owe any money. After all, your good credit is at risk (so they say) and it may seem worth the expense just to get the "creditor" off your back. Don't do it! Write a letter instead. (You may expect a bill from me for this advice.)

In these days of shoddy products, disappearing service, and wrong-side-of-the-looking-glass logic, the reasons to write a good letter of complaint are multitude. We cannot be complacent, because we are at war. We are at war with mediocrity, apathy, and a view of humanity that reduces living, thinking, feeling people to mindless, impotent "consumers." Our enemies are legion and they are big. . . but like Goliath, they can be felled by the little guy. The little guy who writes letters.

It's hard to sit down and compose an effective, reasoned letter, especially when you're mad. And when you're not mad, it's hard to work up the motivation to do it. George Beahm has devised an elegant solution: a selection of model letters to adapt to your specific situation, and as any author can tell you, it's infinitely easier to edit than it is to create.

The model letters serve another function: they keep you from blowing your stack on paper, from reducing your credibility by sounding like a jerk. (In all fairness, there are a lot of true cranks out there that companies have to identify and dismiss as quickly as possible.) The model letters can make sure you're perceived as the sane, reasonable, and determined individual you are.

If you're angry at being a victim, or if you're just tired of being taken for granted, the letters and advice in this book can change your life. Quit being pushed around! Fight back! *Write* back!

Now, you'll have to excuse me. MasterCard has just billed me $177 for a purchase that couldn't possibly be mine. I have to write a letter.

—Jan Strnad
Hollywood, CA

Foreword

In the movie *Back to the Future* actor Michael J. Fox, transported from the 1980s to the 1950s, watches in amazement as a car pulls up to a service station and sets off a flurry of activity: attendants in clean, white uniforms rush out to clean the windshield, check the oil, and fill the gas tank.

How times have changed!

Customer service and satisfaction isn't what it used to be. The philosophy of putting the customer first has changed to putting the customer last.

The Problem Worsens

If you've ever bought a product or service and felt you were taken to the cleaners, don't feel alone. According to the Federal Trade Commission, "buyers are dissatisfied with 75 million purchases a year." According to the 1987 Better Business Bureau's Report, summarizing 1986 data, they handled over two million complaints. In other words, the vast majority of complaints must be an *individual* responsibility; don't expect any agency to know more, care more, or do more than you.

Ironically, consumer dissatisfaction is at an all-time high, at a time when American businesses are in search of excellence using quick fixes with "one minute management" and slick advertising to convince you that the customer comes first. Unfortunately, things don't seem to be improving quickly enough.

A *Washington Post* poll conducted in October 1987 indicated that 45 percent of the adults surveyed felt the quality of service at major department stores was "just fair" or "poor." When asked if they felt the quality of service was getting better or getting worse, 65 percent indicated that it was "getting worse" or "staying the same." The bottom line for businesses: 48 percent of those polled indicated that they had stopped shopping at a particular store because of the problems they experienced.

American businesses are very aware of the public perception. For too long, they've seen market shares, profits, and return on investments

9

erode. Focusing on the fundamental fact that customer satisfaction is of paramount importance, American businesses are reevaluating how to improve customer satisfaction.

Bringing the point home, the Japan Management Association conducted a study with Japanese and U.S. key executives who named the most important elements in their long-range strategic marketing operations. Of those Japanese executives surveyed on improvement of post-sales service and claim-handling procedures, only 4.9 percent considered it a priority, which indicates that they are relatively satisfied with their current level of service. In contrast, an astonishing 39 percent of the U.S. executives felt this critical area had to be targeted as a priority, which indicates they are aware of the problem—the general dissatisfaction of the American consumer with U.S. products and services.

Clearly, American management is taking notice. Why? Because they can't afford *not* to. For this reason, you as a consumer are in an excellent position to have your voice heard and taken seriously.

Goals of this Book

First, I want to show you how to write an effective complaint letter, step-by-step, that will insure you and your problem is given the attention it deserves.

Second, I will provide model letters with explanations on how to customize them to fit your purpose.

Third, I intend to explain what third party assistance is available and tell you what they can and cannot do for you.

Why I Wrote this Book

The majority of books written for consumers only cover preventive action; few discuss what to do after the fact, and even fewer have realistic advice based on personal experience that will, more often than not, work.

The principles I discuss in this book are proven methods that I've used successfully for many years, complaining to small, local firms and large, international firms. Because the principles are universal, they are applicable to virtually anyone in any situation. In the majority of cases, I've gotten what I wanted—an explanation, an apology in writing, credit, refund, or other adjustment.

Why Letters Work

Regardless of whom you contact for help, they'll want to know the facts. Your complaint letter is the best way to present the facts, clearly and succinctly, to everyone who needs to know: the local merchant, customer service at the corporate level, the Better Business Bureau, or to the Judge at Small Claims Court.

While a phone call can be an appropriate vehicle for complaint—if you know exactly what you want to say, who you need to talk to, and document the conservation with written notes, with a copy to the other party—it's far easier to use the phone as a tool for gathering information and leave the details to the complaint letter. In addition, a good complaint letter is proof positive that you are serious about getting satisfaction. A physical object that sits on the desk and demands attention and resolution, a complaint letter can't be ignored forever.

Looking Into the Future

The gap between what companies promise and deliver, or what you think they've promised and what they've delivered, will continue to be a wide one. When you aren't satisfied, let your voice be heard—loud and clear!

Chapter 1

Preventive Measures

The old adage is true: an ounce of prevention is worth a pound of cure. Before and after you buy, make sure you've done everything you can to protect yourself.

Before You Buy

1. *Get impartial recommendations.* Before you go out to buy, be sure to ask your friends about the product, read the leading consumer magazines and buying guides, and shop around locally. Don't let a salesperson force you into making a premature decision; after all, the salesperson doesn't have to live with the purchase—you do.

2. *Don't be in a hurry.* Despite how good a deal it sounds, don't be pressed into buying on the spot.

A friend who was in the market for a new car nearly drove the salesmen crazy at a half-dozen car dealerships with her repeated visits. Armed with information on *every* model she wanted, comparative prices, special offers, and shopping around separately for financing, she finally bought the car of her choice at a fair price, with a good trade-in on her present car, and at competitive financing rates.

Another friend who walked in off the street to a car dealership bought a car that night. He had no intention of making an immediate purchase, but the deal sounded good. He should have taken his time. In retrospect, he had to fight the dealership to delete the credit life insurance he didn't want; he opted for the dealer financing, not realizing it would cost him 3 percent more than he would be charged at the bank; and he didn't get a trade-in on his current car, which he later sold for less than he could have gotten from the dealership.

The moral: shop around and don't let a salesperson intimidate you into buying immediately. You, not the salesman, have to live with your decision.

3. *Deal with reputable merchants.* If you haven't dealt with a specific merchant before, don't assume he is reputable. For starters, ask your friends, family, and neighbors about the company. Then check with the Better Business Bureau, which will read or send a company report to you. Forewarned is forearmed.

4. *Make sure you understand what you are buying.* If you aren't sure, ask questions. *Before* you buy is the time to get your questions answered—not *after,* when you are having problems.

5. *Check the warranty.* Surprisingly, few people take the time to fill out the warranty card and mail it in. The manufacturer's warranty gives you recourse, but only if you are a registered owner.

6. *Read the instruction manual.* Have you ever taken the time to read the instruction manual to your car? You'd be surprised how many people

don't read the instruction pamphlets or manuals that come with their product. In some cases, when they call to complain, the answer can be found in the instruction manual. In addition, the manual normally provides information on maintenance, which should be followed carefully. This is especially important when you are pursuing compensation on a claim. The first point they will bring up: did you operate the product according to the manufacturer's recommendations? Did you inadvertently void the warranty by using the product improperly?

7. *Keep proof of purchase.* If you pay with cash, get a receipt. It's preferable, though, to use a credit card or a personal check because you have proof of purchase and recourse in case the product is defective.

Though rules for credit card purchases vary, the following is typical; look for this in small print in the back of your statement:

> If you have a problem with the quality of goods or services that you purchased with a credit card, and you have tried in good faith to correct the problem with the merchant, you may not have to pay the remaining amount due on the goods or services. You have this protection only when the purchase price was more than $50 and the purchase was made in your home state or within 100 miles of your mailing address. If we mailed you the advertisement for the property or services, all purchases are covered regardless of amount or location of purchase.

When you use a personal check, you can always stop payment, though most banks will want to know why and also charge you a "stop payment" fee, approximately $15-$20. As a courtesy, you should notify the merchant that you've stopped payment and why, since he may consider it a returned check and charge you $15 or $20.

Set Up A File

Though tedious, it's essential that you establish and maintain a file for all paperwork regarding purchases. The easiest way to keep track of everything is to buy an accordion-like file with tabs, available for under $10 at most office supply stores.

Alphabetically by vendor, you should keep in a manila folder copies of all pertinent paperwork: your sales receipt, a photocopy of any warranty paperwork, instruction and operating manual, rebate information, and a product history sheet (see Form 1). By doing so, you can easily retrieve the complete history of any product or service you buy.

In many cases where I've had problems with consumer purchases, having the complete history of the purchase made it easier to get satisfaction. Contrast that to the plight of the person who has no receipts, didn't file the warranty paperwork, and can't remember anything.

After You Buy
1. *Follow instructions for operation of the product.* Remember, improper use or abuse can void the warranty.
2. *Invoke your rights under warranty.* If you aren't sure, ask the salesperson who sold you the product to explain exactly what you are entitled to. Separate from the warranty, an extended maintenance contract also gives you specific rights; these are spelled out in detail in the agreement you sign, for which you usually pay an additional fee.
3. *If you have a problem, contact the dealer immediately.* Don't wait until months go by when you report a problem; procrastination may be taken as a sign by the merchant that you aren't too concerned. If you were, he reasons, why didn't you bring this to our attention earlier?
4. *Use your product history sheet to record actions you've taken.* Being specific—naming names, dates, what was discussed, and what was promised—gives you the benefit of the doubt. In many cases, the merchant will not have as accurate a recollection or record.
5. *Know your options.* Basically, this involves writing a complaint letter to the appropriate person, then being prepared to carry it further if you don't get resolution.

Chapter **2**

Working Within the System

In order to get your complaint resolved, you have to understand your chances of getting satisfaction depend on how well you work within the established system. Your complaint will be taken seriously if it's clear that you've initiated contact at the lowest possible level, then worked your way up the complaint hierarchy.

Keep in mind that your goal is to get your complaint resolved quickly, simply, and satisfactorily with a minimum of effort. You don't want to make a career out of complaining; you just want your complaint resolved.

In order of whom you should contact, I recommend the following:

Helping Yourself
1. Contact the salesperson who sold you the product or service.
2. Contact the customer service department.
3. Contact the store manager or, if necessary, the regional manager.
4. Contact customer service at the corporate level.
5. Contact the president of the company or the CEO, the chief executive officer.

Third Party Help
1. Contact the local media with consumer action hotlines.
2. Contact the Better Business Bureau.
3. Contact third party industry consumer programs.
4. Contact third party dispute resolution programs.
5. Contact the state consumer office.
6. Contact the Federal consumer office.

Legal Help
1. Legal aid or legal services
2. Private attorneys
3. Small claims court

Your goal, of course, should be to get your problem resolved as quickly and easily as possible, which means that you should be prepared to handle the matter yourself unless third-party help or legal assistance is essential to get satisfactory resolution.

Pros and Cons
The Salesperson
The salesperson is the logical person whom you should contact, since he is most familiar with what was promised and, presumably, your expectations. Unfortunately, salespeople are at the bottom of a hierarchy and, depending on the company, may not be able to handle anything but the most ordinary problems. If the situation involves changing policy, or

even modifying it slightly to satisfy you, the salesperson may not have that option.

Case in point: A friend went to buy a car and declined the credit life insurance; however, the business manager showed him the car contract and, having folded it so that it could not be fully reviewed, told my friend where to sign, which he did. Consequently, he "signed" for insurance.

Later, when reviewing all the paperwork, my friend saw that he had "requested" credit life insurance. He immediately complained to the salesman, who shrugged his shoulders and said, "I can't do anything." As it turned out, the business manager who instigated this little deception told the customer that "a contract's a contract," then told my friend to forget it. My friend is nothing if not persistent and, after checking around found out from the bank officer that after the sale, the credit life could be canceled, which he promptly did. The business manager, forced to comply, claimed after the fact that "there was a communications problem."

The key point: the salesman had little or no authority, and if my friend had taken his word at it, he would still be paying an exorbitant amount for credit life insurance that he didn't need, didn't want, and didn't request.

The Customer Service Department

The customer service department can be helpful, but again, like the salesman, they may not have a lot of options on how to handle your complaint. Chances are good that they operate within specific guidelines from which they can't deviate. The key thing to remember is that, like the salesman, these people do not represent management; *only at management level can policies be modified or changed within reason.*

The Store Manager or Regional Manager

At this level you have reached management, but it's at the local and regional level. While previous contacts can be made in person or by phone, your initial contact with the store manager should be by letter. The chances are good that you will have to summarize what has transpired to date, and a letter is the best way to update.

In most cases, even if you were to take the complaint higher in the corporate structure, you'd find that they'd delegate down to the store manager or his staff. For this reason, it's important to provide him with all the necessary information to evaluate your claim. Similarly, the district manager is a member of management and, as such, can make a decision that can be implemented at local level.

In the best companies, the authority to satisfy the customer is delegated to the lowest possible level. You can learn a lot about a company's commitment to customer service by merely observing how far up the ladder you have to go to get your complaint heard and acted upon in a fair and impartial manner. The higher up you go, the greater the possibility that the company doesn't practice what it preaches.

As Paul Hawken, writing in *Growing a Business,* says:

> Management sees customers as an entity "outside" the company, and this is especially true in the case of the big corporations and retailers. Businesses are armed to the teeth to prevent fraud, abuse, hassles, and ripoffs coming from customers or suppliers. They have elaborate procedures for dealing with anything that might go wrong in the area of service. Meanwhile, and not coincidentally, just about everything has gone wrong with American business. *No developed country in the world offers such miserable care and service to its customers.* [Italics mine.]

The tip-off: the simpler the guarantee, the easier the company makes it on you by giving you the benefit of the doubt, the greater the possibility that service is not merely a slogan but a working philosophy. Zone VI, a small company that manufactures specialized equipment for the serious photographer, has a simple guarantee: "If any item marked with my initials [FP for Fred Picker] ever fails to perform its designated function for any reason (except battery replacement, drowning, gratuitous abuse or internal tampering), we will repair or replace it free of charge."

Fred Picker, owner of Zone VI, has said repeatedly that, "Nobody ever got stuck with anything bought from Zone VI. Nobody ever will."

The President or CEO

The president or chief executive officer is your final court of appeal within a company's hierarchy. Ultimately, the buck stops here. Because he is the last court of appeal, be sure you've gone through the right channels below his level so that you've appealed to everyone, *then* progressed to the next level.

In many cases the president, who is typically insulated by a legion of people, doesn't know what his customers really think; he may rely on his staff to provide him with information, or he may read reports from his departments. While a complaint letter written to him may be handled by his executive secretary, chances are good that, having come from the head office, your complaint letter will have more impact because everyone in the organization knows management is aware of the problem and is involved, or will get involved if the customer is not satisfied.

In cases where I've written to presidents, I've always gotten a response.

In some cases, my complaint is sent back down to the local manager with a note to take care of the problem. In other cases, I don't hear directly, but I hear from a customer service department or staff person who tells me he's gotten the letter from the head office and has been instructed to act accordingly. In a few cases, the president responds but indicates his people were right in their assessment of the situation, at which point you have the option of taking it to a third party.

There's a growing realization among businesses, large and small alike, that *how the customer perceives them* is the key to a good customer service program. Today, more than ever, the customer *can't* be taken for granted. For this reason, your polite but firm complaint letter is the quickest and best way for you to get what you want. The chances are good that, so long as your request is reasonable, you won't have to take your complaint any further.

Third Party Help

If you don't feel like going at it alone, there are many sources of free third-party help that can assist you. Obviously, the complaint letter sent to the appropriate people at a local, regional, or national level shows that you've done everything you can to resolve the problem on your own. In many cases, assuming the company isn't out to rip you off, the complaint letters will be sufficient.

There are, though, circumstances where you might want third-party assistance. In cases of large-ticket items, like cars or major appliances, and in cases where the circumstances are very complicated and can't adequately be respresented in a letter, you may want a helping hand.

In addition, there are companies out there that operate without ethics. Their attitude is, simply, "I've made the sale, so screw you." These companies operate on the assumption that there's always another sucker out there, another ignorant customer who doesn't know his rights, or that there are plenty of people who aren't going to complain or fight; they'll just go away.

In these instances, third-party assistance can be very valuable. Able to evaluate your situation objectively and separate fact from fiction, able to give you background information or specific information about a company or your rights as a consumer, third-party assistance can get involved without being personally involved, as you are.

Consumer Action Hotlines with Local Media

There's no question that local media can be very effective in getting a straight answer from a stubborn merchant who, in effect, has told you to forget it. A local newspaper columnist, a radio talk-show host, or TV reporter always has the exposure value of the media to use as a leverage to get action.

On the other hand, because of the volume of requests received, chances are good that they will only help you if it can be quickly resolved with a phone call or letter, if it's typical of what their other readers might be experiencing, or if it's a severe problem that they feel needs the additional clout of the media.

In cases where consumers have gone directly to the media and complained without giving the merchant a chance to speak for himself, ill will can result. *Always give the merchant a chance to correct the problem.* Then, if he won't or doesn't correct the problem, you've got recourse.

Don't make the mistake of assuming that the media knows more than you about what to do on how to complain for results. In a letter to Ann Landers, a faithful reader of thirty years wrote and complained about defective appliances. "All these products were made in the U.S.A. Any advice for me and thousands of others who are experiencing the same agony?"

Ann Landers concluded: "What can we do about it? Nothing. Go fight city hall." While Landers did suggest contacting the appliance manufacturer's service center with a toll-free number, no other guidance was given. What Landers could have suggested was contacting an industry third-party dispute resolution program that assists consumers after contacts with the manufacturer have not been productive. MACAP, Major Appliance Consumer Action Panel, has a toll-free number (1-800-621-0477) with a recorded message explaining that if you continue to have problems with the manufacturer, contact them with a letter and complete details, at which point they will assess the situation and may help you.

The Better Business Bureau

Supported by the business community, the Better Business Bureau, commonly known as the BBB, has for seventy years acted as an impartial third party seeking to assist consumers and businesses alike by resolution through open communication, mediation, and arbitration.

Like other third-party groups, BBB requires that before they get involved, you should try to resolve the complaint directly with the merchant who sold you the product or service. If that does not work, then they will assist you, depending on the nature of the claim. (See chapter 6 for a detailed explanation on what the BBB can and cannot do for you.)

Third Party Industry Consumer Programs:
Trade Associations

Almost every major industry maintains a trade association that, among other things, wants to present a good public image. These programs will mediate disputes between you and the company, but only after you have complained to the individual business and its corporate headquarters.

Third Party Dispute Resolution Programs
Established by major industry, these programs will try and help you resolve a complaint. Among these is the Better Business Bureau's National Consumer Arbitration Program.

Consumer Protection Offices
Part of state, county, or city governments, consumer protection offices can provide publications, offer information, or assist in resolving complaints.

Federal Agencies
All federal consumer agencies can provide information and also handle major areas of consumer complaints. Although you càn contact the headquarters, it is preferable to work through local offices first.

Directories
The *Consumer's Resource Handbook,* a publication of the Office of Consumer Affairs, offers a consumer assistance directory listing:
• Corporate consumer contacts
• Automobile manufacturers corporate contacts
• Better Business Bureaus
• Industry third-party dispute resolution programs
• Trade associations
• State, county, and city government consumer protection offices
• Various state agencies (banking authorities, commissions and offices on aging, insurance regulators, utility commissions, weights and measures offices)
• Federal Agencies and Offices
Available for free copies may be obtained by writing to: *Handbook,* Consumer Information Center, Pueblo, Colorado 81009.

Legal Help
When all else fails, legal options are always available. Depending on the nature of your complaint and your financial resources, you can seek satisfaction through the courts.
Legal Aid and Legal Services offices are available to people who can't afford to hire private attorneys, so long as they meet financial eligibility requirements. The legal services are free, funded by state, local, or

private funding or by local bar associations.

What they do: According to the *Consumer's Resource Handbook,* these offices can handle "problems such as landlord-tenant, credit, utilities, family issues such as divorce and adoption, social security, welfare, unemployment, and worker's compensation." Depending on the office, and the board of directors, priorities are set and determinations are made on the kinds of cases handled. In those cases, they usually refer you to other organizations that can help.

Private Attorneys

Because going to civil court is expensive and time-consuming, even when you have a case that is warranted, you should consider other options before hiring a private attorney to represent your interests.

Private attorneys normally charge by the hour ($50 and up in major metropolitan areas), by a contingency fee (you pay only if you win, but if you lose you pay court costs), or by a predetermined percentage of the amount involved plus court costs.

If you feel your problem is serious and you want legal aid, an initial consultation, usually available for free or for a nominal fee, will give you the chance to discuss the merits of your case.

One alternative is to contact a legal clinic, which has become a popular option for people who want a quick, low-cost source for legal advice for standard legal matters. Because lawyers can now advertise, you can find them in the Yellow Pages. Some areas also have a lawyer referral service (see the Yellow Pages). But the best way to find a lawyer is to ask friends who are satisfied with their attorneys or, failing that, ask around among your professional acquaintances.

Small Claims Court

If you want legal recourse and want to keep it out of civil court, which can be expensive and time-consuming, you may want to consider small claims court.

Small claims court is where the little guy can have his day in court, with the full power of the law behind him if he wins. Unlike civil court, small claims court offers many advantages:

1. You can expect your case to be heard without long delays.

2. You can represent yourself; an attorney need not be present. (In some states, attorneys are prohibited from small claims court.)

3. You work within a very simple framework, unencumbered by legal gobbledygook and elaborate procedures for presenting your case.

Because of its simplicity, small claims court gives you an inexpensive, quick legal option that can bring you satisfaction.

Case in point: A friend nearly talked herself hoarse complaining to a number of people about a security deposit of several hundred dollars that she couldn't recoup after she left the apartment. The company that took her deposit had sold out to another company, who claimed they didn't owe anything to her. After writing one complaint letter—mailed by certified mail, return receipt requested—she waited two weeks and then filed a claim in small claims court. As soon as the company was served papers, *they* contacted my friend and offered to pay the full amount in question immediately.

In her case, the *threat* of going to court was sufficient because the company that tried to renege on its legal obligation knew it was in the wrong and that, if the case went to court, it would lose anyway and suffer bad public relations in the process.

Remember, third party assistance should be used when you have expended reasonable effort through working with a company and its chain of command. Only after that proves fruitless should you ask for outside help. In many cases, especially on routine matters, the complaint letter will get action. But know your options in case you have to use them: third party help and legal recourse.

Chapter **3**

Common Consumer Mistakes

When you have a legitimate complaint and call, write, or visit a merchant in person, you are asking for his assistance in helping you. Keeping that in mind, it's clear that negative behavior on your part will only turn a potential ally into a bitter enemy.

Rule #1: Be professional in how you present yourself and your problem.

Case in point: A few years ago I was in a laundromat when a customer stormed in, slammed the door, and went straight to a clerk and let loose with both barrels. In a loud voice—loud enough so everyone in the establishment could hear—the customer complained that the laundromat personnel were incompetent, that they ruined his clothes because they didn't give a damn, that he was going to "alert the press" who he felt would run a story about this shoddy establishment, and that court action was a real possibility—unless he got what he wanted!

Having worked in retail as a salesman and store manager, I can imagine how the poor clerk felt. She stood and took the abuse, then tried to point out she had nothing to do with the problem in question, at which point the man laid into her again, citing the stupidity of management, the loss he suffered, and the hell he would bring down on the business in general. Having worked himself up in a frenzy, nearly foaming at the mouth, he stormed out, muttering loudly and cursing on his way out the door. I was tempted to yell out to him, "Don't let the door hit you on the way out!" but it wasn't my store and I kept silent.

Whatever the merits of the case might be, the unhappy man did nothing to help himself by verbally raising hell with the store clerk, when in fact his complaint should have been addressed to the store manager. In addition, having alienated and insulted the store clerk thoroughly, in the presence of everyone else in the store, did he honestly think she would do anything to help him? Finally, even if he goes to see the store manager later, or if he writes to complain, the store manager is going to remember that his employee was abused and humiliated, so why should he go out of his way to satisfy the jerk?

My recommendation: use common sense and treat people with dignity; focus on the issue, not the people. Most importantly, don't lose your temper and become your own worst enemy by going on the offensive and threatening the store manager and his people; if you want to back up your claims with legal action, you can always take him to small claims court.

The customer is always right, a maxim many businesses quote. In truth, it's generally good business to let the customer get his way; however, when the customer is wrong, when the customer is abusive and hostile, he's *not* right, and chances are good the merchant won't make any attempt to satisfy him or her. In short, put yourself in the store

28

manager's position; think about how you'd like to be approached and what would work with you, then proceed in an organized and intelligent fashion. Don't assume that store managers or their personnel respond well to threats; they've come to learn that people who loudly complain and make excessive threats are bullies that usually bluff their way through life. What *does* concern the store manager is the reasonable consumer who knows his rights and, if necessary, is prepared to go up the chain of command to seek resolution and, in the end, will use available legal options if necessary.

Rule #2: Don't use the phone to complain.

Because many people are more comfortable with the phone, there is a tendency to pick it up and start talking, without any thought of what you want to say. This is especially true if you have a complaint. Working without any notes, you call and get a receptionist, a secretary, a clerk, an individual in the customer service department, all of whom *do not* have the power to help you. At best, they can refer you to someone who *does* have discretionary power; but by themselves they may be powerless to provide instant answers, make decisions, or change policies.

The best use of the phone is as a tool for gathering information. If you have a complaint and want it to go to a person who can make a decision, rather than working your way through a series of people, explaining your story again and again, simply ask: "I have a problem and would like to speak to someone in charge." Then, after talking briefly with that person, get his name, title, and mailing address and follow-up with a complaint letter.

The other disadvantage in using the phone is that there is no record of your call; you can't prove what was said, unless you document the major points of the conversation on the Product History sheet (see page 31), or you've made notes and provided a copy to the person you spoke with, with a request that if there is any error in what was written, based on the phone call, please write back to clarify the point.

The letter should be simple, direct, and to-the-point like the sample below:

current date ──●	5 January 1988
name, title, and address ──●	Ms. Sue Jackson Manager, Credit Department "Honest Joe's" Car Emporium 302 Main Street Anytown, VA 23666
Subject of letter ──●	Subject: Our phone call of 4 January 1988
Letter to ──●	Dear Ms. Jackson,
A recap of what was discussed ──●	Yesterday you discussed with me on the phone the problems I was having with the billing error. As I indicated to you, I am being billed for a car payment to your company that is in fact not mine; the late payment I was being dunned for is from another individual with the same name in a different city.
The promises made by other party ──●	You promised to do the following: 1. Check your records to find the correct billing address for the other individual with the same name. 2. Change your records to insure all future billings and late notices go to the other individual. 3. Check with your credit department to insure my credit rating hasn't suffered by the inclusion of erroneous data. 4. Notify me within three days from the phone call that the problem has been cleared up, and that I should not expect any further billings. Thank you. Sincerely, Mr. John Smith cc: files

PRODUCT HISTORY:

1. Date
2. Person contacted
3. Subject discussed
4. Resolution

PRODUCT HISTORY

Product/Service: _____

Model Number: _____

Serial Number: _____

PURCHASE INFORMATION:

Salesperson:

Store Address/Phone number:

FINANCIAL:

Cash purchase _____ (Proof of purchase: sales receipt)

Check _____ (Proof of purchase: sales receipt, canceled check)

Credit Card _____ (Proof of purchase: sales receipt, credit card receipt, and itemized account on monthly statement)

DATES:

Purchase date:

Warranty mailed in:

Warranty expires:

Maintenance agreement expires:

SAMPLE, PRODUCT HISTORY

Date, Person Contacted, Subject Discussed, Resolution:

5 Jan 88, in-store visit; salesman, Mr. Robert Hines; bought ATME Tape Recorder with 30-day warranty.

6 Jan 88, tried product at home, but it was defective; the tape recorder would not "fast forward."

7 Jan 88, called Robert Hines, who told me to bring it back for a refund, with all the original packing and the sales receipt.

10 Jan 88, returned the product with packing and sales receipt; exchanged the ATME Tape Recorder for a replacement.

How Not to Write a Complaint Letter

If you want to be taken seriously, instead of being dismissed as a crank or a fool, exercise common sense in writing a complaint letter. Don't use the letter as a vehicle to vent your frustration, since that isn't the time or the place. Instead, use it as a vehicle to present you and your case in the best light.

Here are some pitfalls to avoid:

1. Don't use obscenity in the letter. (It makes you look like an idiot out of control.)

2. Don't be vague in what you are trying to say. (Get to the point and state your case clearly.)

3. Don't be disorganized in writing the letter. (You should use a standard format for writing the letter, modeled after the sample letters I've provided.)

4. Don't make threats you can't carry out. (If legal recourse is your only option, then don't jump the gun and say: "I'll take you to court!")

5. Don't use slander or libel the company. (Don't say: "You are a crooked thief!"

6. Don't carbon the world. Keep a carbon for yourself, since you may have to share it with other people who may have to help you get your case taken seriously, but don't pepper your letter with dozens of organizations because it dilutes your effort and marks you as an amateur. Even if you carbon only two organizations, both may decline to get involved on the grounds that the *other* organization may be working on the problem and why duplicate effort?

7. Don't write long letters. Most problems can be adequately stated on one page, two at most. People don't have time to read long letters, so get to the point.

8. Don't forget to keep a copy of anything you write. (If someone else has the only copy, how do you know what you've written?)

Here's an example of how *not* to write a complaint letter:

23 January 1988

No name
for ———————• The President
follow-up   Attila B. Hun Motor Corp.
    2303 Main Street
    Anytown, USA 29244

Insulting ——————• Dear Brain-Damaged Member of Management,

opinion,   I swear I've never seen such incompetence in all my
not fact ——————• life! After buying one of your worthless cars, then
    having to take it in for repair after repair, you people
    can't seem to get anything right.

profanity ——————• Damn it, I paid good money and expect to get what
accusatory   I paid for. What's the matter with you guys, anyway?

threat ——————• Listen, if you can't fix the car like you said you
libelous   would, you crook, I'll see you in court!
statement

    Angrily Yours,

    Mr. John Smith

overkill ——————• cc: Better Business Bureau, local Chamber of
    Commerce, Ralph Nader, *Washington Post*, CEO
    of Hun Motor Corporation, President of the United
    States.

The same letter, rewritten in a positive light.

23 January 1988

Send to
specific ——————• Mr. John Toole
individual   Attila B. Hun Motor Corp.
                    2303 Main Street
                    Anytown, USA 29244

                    Dear Mr. Toole,

Specific, to-   On 14 January 1988 I bought on installment credit a
the-point, —————• 1985, two-door, Zephr Classic. Despite the claims
and factual   that the car was in good shape, my mechanic
                    looked over the car and notified me that the brake
                    linings were worn, at which point Mr. John Smith in
                    your service department agreed to fix it for free.

The situation   I've taken it to him twice, and the problem is still not
and the ————————• resolved. I don't know why I am having a continuing
expectation   problem, but I would appreciate it if you were to look
with a dead-   into it and get the problem fixed. The car otherwise
line stated   runs well, and I would expect you to stand behind
                    this car just as you have the other cars I've bought
                    from you over the years. Can you call me within the
                    week to let me know what you will do?

                    Sincerely,

                    Mr. John Smith

docu- ——————————• cc: files
mentation

Chapter **4**

How To Mail A Complaint Letter

Where to Send Your Letter

The letter will be effective only if you send it to the right person—the individual that has been identified to you as having the power and authority to help you solve your problem.

Common mistakes include:

1. Sending a letter to the wrong person. (You want to send your letter to the person who can help you; avoid sending a letter to a clerk or low-level manager. In order, you should send it to the manager of the complaint department (customer service), the store manager or the regional manager, and then to corporate headquarters.

2. Sending a letter to the right person, but not using his name. Sending a letter to the store manager is far less effective than Mr. Joe Smith, the store manager.

3. Sending copies of the letter to third parties before the recipient has had a chance to respond. Obviously, as a matter of courtesy, you should give your recipient the opportunity to resolve your complaint. I would recommend your waiting at least a week, possibly two. Then, if no action is forthcoming, you can take the matter up with someone at a higher level.

Third parties who get a copy of a complaint letter will not take any action, unless they know you've already gotten a negative response and need additional help. Simply carboning them at this point is premature, since they will be waiting to see what results you've achieved on your own.

4. Sending a letter to the president first. Because the president is the last court of appeal within his organization, should the president respond unfavorably to your letter, his people down the line will not buck him by coming to your aid. Start at the lowest level, then work your way up; appeal to each level and escalate if necessary. By working within the system, you'll find that if your complaint is reasonable, it can be handled at the lowest levels instead of writing to the president who, in most cases, will turn it over to the local manager for resolution.

Work *within* the system to resolve your complaint; after you've done everything you can within the system and did not get satisfactory resolution, then go *outside* the system.

Preparing the Envelope

If you have a business letterhead, use it if your complaint is company business; if the complaint is personal, then use a personal letterhead or blank paper and matching envelope.

When addressing the envelope, you should avoid marking it personal or confidential unless the contents should not be shared with anyone else. In most cases, however, a complaint letter is a business letter; there is no need to mark the envelope as confidential.

Your address should look like the address below:

name of recipient ⟶●	Mr. Attila B. Hun
job title ⟶●	Manager, Customer Relations
company name ⟶●	Hun Motor Company, Inc.
street address ⟶●	4302 Steppe Road
city, state, and zip ⟶●	Hampton, VA 23666

Preparing the Letter

I use the full block style when writing letters, in which all lines are flush with the left margin and there are no indentations.

If you are not using letterhead stationery, your letter will look like this:

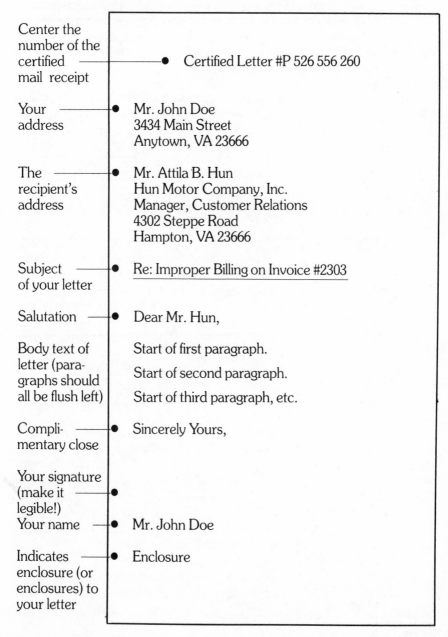

Center the number of the certified mail receipt —————● Certified Letter #P 526 556 260

Your ————● Mr. John Doe
address   3434 Main Street
                   Anytown, VA 23666

The ————● Mr. Attila B. Hun
recipient's   Hun Motor Company, Inc.
address   Manager, Customer Relations
                   4302 Steppe Road
                   Hampton, VA 23666

Subject ————● Re: Improper Billing on Invoice #2303
of your letter

Salutation ————● Dear Mr. Hun,

Body text of   Start of first paragraph.
letter (para-
graphs should   Start of second paragraph.
all be flush left)
                  Start of third paragraph, etc.

Compli- ————● Sincerely Yours,
mentary close

Your signature
(make it ————●
legible!)
Your name ————● Mr. John Doe

Indicates ————● Enclosure
enclosure (or
enclosures) to
your letter

Documentation

Sam Goldwyn once remarked, "An oral agreement isn't worth the paper it's printed on." If you want proof, as the saying goes, get it in writing!

The single biggest mistake people make is that, for whatever reasons, they don't have the proper documentation to substantiate the claim. With the right documentation, you've got a convincing case; without it, you are leaving everything open to interpretation.

Oral Documentation

Obviously, unless you use a tape recorder, you don't have an exact record of what was said. To make sure that what you've agreed upon is accurate, especially on matters that are very detailed or promises made that aren't in writing, protect yourself by writing a letter covering key points and mailing it to the other person.

The military calls this a memorandum of understanding; businesses call it a letter of intent, when promises are made and everything must be clearly defined. In both instances, the purpose is simple: to have a written record of what was discussed.

A lawyer advised me that the best way to protect yourself is to write the letter of record, mail it by certified mail, return receipt requested, and keep a copy. The letter should indicate the specifics discussed, and also indicate that if there are any changes or any other interpretations, the recipient should respond in writing. Otherwise, it is assumed the letter adequately covers the subject discussed.

Lawyers are trained to plug up every loophole, but they have a point: don't leave anything subject to interpretation.

As a matter of practicality, you can take notes and keep them on hand, or record the subjects discussed on the Product History sheet. *Don't leave it to memory!* The memory grows old, forgets, and then you are depending on someone *else* to refresh your memory.

On consumer problems, chances are that you'll have phone conversations, conversations in person with various people, and activity through the mail. If you document this, your recollection will be substantial and authoritative. Chances are the company you are dealing with does *not* keep such close tabs, unless it is a finance company, in which case it keeps a running account of all letters, phone calls, and contacts with you. (I know because I've dealt with credit card companies that keep meticulous records—and can cite them, reading off their computer.)

Make sure *you* have a record of what has transpired.

Remember, in any written or telephonic contact, you've got to keep track of the 5 "W"s: who, what, when, where, and why. Also, be sure to indicate what had been promised.

A complaint log is a historical record of what has happened between you and the merchant. All activity should be noted: phone calls, letters, and visits. Be sure to be specific on who you talked to, when, by which means, what was discussed, promises made, and follow-up action promised or necessary on your part. (You'd be surprised how often people promise to follow-up and, for whatever reasons, don't.)

I had an instance where a national finance company sent me dunning letters because I missed a car payment. The problem, of course, was not of my making; I hadn't financed a car through them, but they sent it to me in error due to an incorrect address provided to them from the post office. My complaint log looked like this:

ACTIVITY LOG

Subject: Erroneous billing

1. 2-15-88, received from Hun Motor Corporation a bill of $295 plus interest for a late car payment.

2. On 2-16-88, I contacted the account representative and explained that I wasn't the individual in question, that I didn't have a car financed through them, and that I'd like them to immediately stop sending me dunning letters, which I felt might automatically be filed as a late payment on my credit report.

Mrs. John Doe indicated that I must be the right person because the post office provided the mailing address. And after all, people *do* move and don't leave forwarding addresses. I countered that on the bill itself was a phone number that was not mine; it belonged to the person who *should* have gotten the bill.

She refused to stop sending the collection letters because she thought I was lying.

3. On 2-17-88, I wrote a certified letter, return receipt requested, to the president of the finance company.

4. On 2-25-88, I received a letter of apology from him and on 2-27-88, I received a phone call from the local manager who apologized profusely. She promised to check and see if any bad credit

---

information had been sent to credit bureaus. She promised to call me back within a week.

5. On 2-30-88, she called back and told me no negative information had been filed. She reassured me this wouldn't happen again.

Some Comments

The situation I've outlined is a fairly common occurrence. The names, obviously, had been changed to protect the guilty. The problem had been resolved quickly because in my letter to the president of the finance company at corporate headquarters, I included my complaint log; he was able to read it quickly, make a few phone calls, check my story out, and verify everything was in fact what I had stated.

He then immediately apologized in a letter, and instructed the local branch manager to do likewise by phone. Key point: without all the information, this matter could have dragged on. If you want *timely* resolution, provide full details and make it easy on the company to resolve your problem.

Paper documentation

You'd be surprised how often people throw away essential paperwork, even on large-ticket items. True, the paperwork can accumulate, but if you throw it away, you have no record and must rely on someone *else* to provide it.

Here's a checklist of what you should always keep on hand, preferably in an accordion-file in a separate envelope to make it easy to file and retrieve paperwork:

Proof of sale:
1. credit card receipt
2. credit card monthly statement
3. canceled check (photocopy *both* sides when showing proof of sale)
4. invoice or bill marked "paid"
5. sales receipt (cash register form)

Supportive paperwork
1. estimate form
2. contract
3. warranty paperwork (send in warranty form, photocopy for your records, and file with warranty agreement)

4. bill or invoice
5. purchase order
6. written correspondence (letters, notes, memos)
7. record of oral conversation (complaint log or activity log)

Protecting Yourself

Make sure you keep all paperwork where you can retrieve it easily. Make sure you do not give your original paperwork to anyone. If they need to see it, fine; show it. But if they want to keep it, tell them to make a photocopy and return the original.

In every instance where a claim is made, having all the paperwork is the best ammunition you have. Without it, you might get partial or no satisfaction after a period of unnecessary delay.

Proof of Delivery

If you want legal proof of delivery, you will have to pay extra for having your first-class letter sent by certified mail, return receipt requested. The costs involved are nominal, but it's legal proof of delivery—cheap insurance.

At this writing (3 April 1988) the charges involved for mailing a one-ounce letter work out like this:

first class postage (1 ounce)	$0.25
certified mail	$0.85
return receipt requested	$0.90
TOTAL	$2.00

Obviously, if it weighs more than an ounce, the postage will cost a bit more. Also, if you want the return receipt to show additional information beyond a signature showing receipt of the letter, there are additional charges.

Forms Needed

Available at your local post office for free, get two dozen PS Form 3800 (Receipt for Certified Mail) and a similar quantity of PS Form 3811 (Domestic Return Receipt).

44

Postal Service Form 3800

receipt number ———•

recipient ———•

first class postage (1 ounce) ———•

fee for certified mail ———•

return receipt fee ———•

total charges ———•

post office postmark with stamp ———•

detachable receipt affixed to the mailed piece ———•

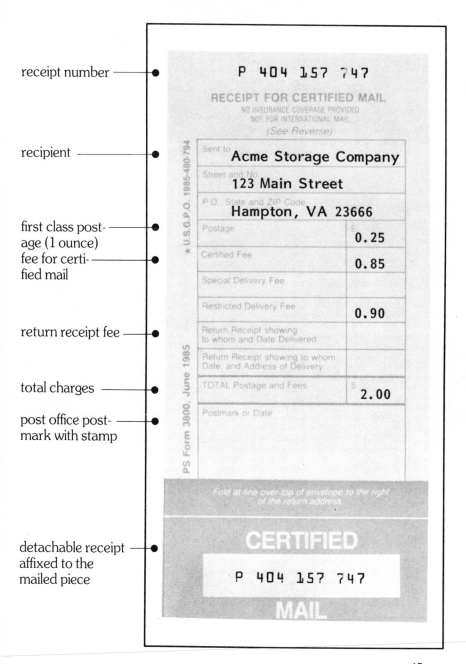

P 404 157 747

RECEIPT FOR CERTIFIED MAIL
NO INSURANCE COVERAGE PROVIDED
NOT FOR INTERNATIONAL MAIL
(See Reverse)

Sent to **Acme Storage Company**

Street and No **123 Main Street**

P.O., State and ZIP Code **Hampton, VA 23666**

Postage **0.25**

Certified Fee **0.85**

Special Delivery Fee

Restricted Delivery Fee **0.90**

Return Receipt showing to whom and Date Delivered

Return Receipt showing to whom, Date, and Address of Delivery

TOTAL Postage and Fees **2.00**

Postmark or Date

Fold at line over top of envelope to the right of the return address

CERTIFIED

P 404 157 747

MAIL

* U.S.G.P.O. 1985-480-794

PS Form 3800, June 1985

The front side of a first-class letter, certified mail

CERTIFIED

P 526 556 250

MAIL

RETURN RECEIPT REQUESTED

Mr. Bob Jones
General Manager
Acme Storage
123 Main Street
Hampton, VA 23666

Mr. John Doe
120 Main Street
Anytown, USA 20201

The back side of a first-class letter, with return receipt requested

Back side of a return receipt form, PS 3811

tape

Front side of PS Form 3811:
Return Receipt Requested

Back side of PS Form 3811:
Return Receipt Requested

SENDER: Complete items 1 and 2 when additional services are desired, and complete items 3 and 4.
Put your address in the "RETURN TO" Space on the reverse side. Failure to do this will prevent this card from being returned to you. The return receipt fee will provide you the name of the person delivered to and the date of delivery. For additional fees the following services are available. Consult postmaster for fees and check box(es) for additional service(s) requested.

1. ☐ Show to whom delivered, date, and addressee's address. 2. ☐ Restricted Delivery
   ↑(Extra charge)↑   ↑(Extra charge)↑

3. Article Addressed to:

Mr. Grady Blaylock
President
PRMA, POB 6497
Newport News, VA 23606

4. Article Number

P 664 309 128

Type of Service:
☐ Registered   ☐ Insured
☒ Certified   ☐ COD
☐ Express Mail

Always obtain signature of addressee or agent and DATE DELIVERED.

8. Addressee's Address (ONLY if requested and fee paid)

5. Signature — Addressee
X

6. Signature — Agent
X *Ana Taylor*

7. Date of Delivery
3-9-88

PS Form **3811**, Mar. 1987   ★ U.S.G.P.O. 1987-178-268   **DOMESTIC RETURN RECEIPT**

Chapter **5**

How to Write A Complaint Letter

As a customer, you represent lifetime purchases of $140,000 to your car dealer if you are brand loyal; the figure goes up if you count referrals, word of mouth recommendations that get someone else to buy because of your satisfaction. At your local grocery store, you represent $4,400 a year and, over the next five years, $22,000. No matter how you look at it, you as the customer wield the economic hammer; you vote with your buying dollar. Your satisfaction, initially and subsequently, translates to profits; your dissatisfaction translates to a drop in profits. A company knows that it must get you as a customer and, afterward, *keep* you; otherwise, it is providing its competition with your business.

Obviously, in most complaint situations, you hold a lot more power than you realize. Surprisingly, few people complain. According to the Federal Trade Commission, only 4 percent of the customers who are unhappy complain; the rest suffer in silence and take their business elsewhere.

In cases where you *do* complain, you'd be surprised at the results. A Ralph Nader study indicated that 56.5 percent of those who voiced complaints got satisfaction; another survey, by Coca Cola, indicated that "more than 85 percent of those complaints received by the Corporate Consumer Affairs Department are resolved to the consumer's satisfaction." The leading third-party consumer complaint handler, the Better Business Bureau, stated in its 1987 report that "for all presented complaints, the BBB Settlement Index was 76.5 percent."

Clearly, the single biggest reason people are unhappy as customers is that they *don't* complain, possibly because they think it's too much bother; it won't do any good; they don't know what to say or how to say it; or they don't know who to say it to.

The Four-step Process in Complaining

Stripped to its essentials, a good complaint letter requires four steps in writing:

Step 1: *Determine who should get the letter.* As I have explained earlier, you should direct your letter to the person you have identified that can help you resolve your problem or, if necessary, provide you with a name or contact at a higher level who can make policy, change it, or amend it.

Here's where the phone can be used effectively. Start at the lowest level and work your way up. Work *within* the organization, then if necessary work *outside* the organization; and finally, if there is no recourse, work within the legal system.

Within the organization, talk to the person who sold you the product or service, the departmental manager, the store manager, the district manager, the complaint department at corporate headquarters, and finally the president of the company.

Outside the organization, you can contact the Better Business Bureau, a third-party dispute resolution program, an industry consumer program, or the city/county/state consumer office.

Within the legal system, use small claims court or a private attorney to bring to bear the power of the court on your behalf.

The truth is that, if your complaint letter is effective and sent through the channels in proper order, *at some level there will be someone who can, and will, help you.* Consider the statistics:

Inside the organization at corporate level, 85 percent of those customers who complained to Coca Cola were satisfied.

Outside the organization, working through the Better Business Bureau, the settlement index is 76.5 percent.

Inside the legal system, your complaint *must* be responded to; it cannot be effectively ignored. In the system, the relative merits of the case are discussed and, in the end, the judge makes a legally binding decision.

Step 2: *Outline your letter.* Don't sit down and dash off a quick letter, hoping it will work. Remember, you are presenting your case on paper; be sure you help yourself by presenting your case in an organized and professional manner that makes it easy for the recipient to make a quick decision on what needs to be done to satisfy you.

After reviewing the 14 sample complaint letters, choose the one that most likely fits your situation, then change the wording on the specifics of your case to describe your situation.

Also, don't write an angry letter. You aren't going to win anyone by being rude, abusive, insulting, and by showing your command of profanity.

Step 3. *Write you letter using a step-by-step approach.* The key is presenting your information in an organized fashion; the facts will speak loudly if told simply and in a direct manner.

Step 4. Review you letter to *make sure you haven't forgotten anything.*

The key point to keep in mind is that, when writing a letter, you are asking for help. You are appealing to someone who presumably is in a position to help you. You are looking for a "win-win" outcome in which you are satisfied and the merchant is satisfied, too: You want your complaint handled quickly, and the merchant wants to satisfy you and keep your business.

Points to Cover in Your Letter

The organization of your letter should present your case in a simple and direct fashion. Generally, you can keep your complaint letter to one page, even with letterhead; in some cases, two pages will be necessary, which is fine if you strive for conciseness. Your letter will have a powerful effect on the reader if its general appearance is professional, if the content accurately reflects your position, if the letter is organized so that it can be followed in logical fashion, and if your documentation supports what you've said in the body of the letter.

In virtually every case, your letter will have to address eight key points to make a case. These are as follows:

1. What is the problem?
2. What impact has the problem had on you?
3. What is your history as a customer with the merchant?
4. Why does the problem exist?
5. Who do you feel is responsible for causing the problem?
6. What have you done to correct the problem?
7. What actions do you want taken to correct the problem?
8. When do you expect a response?

1. What is the problem?

According to the Better Business Bureau, the ten most common complaints, ranked in descending order, are as follows:

1. Unsatisfactory service, not related to repairs, on "the inadequacy of business performance in such matters as installation, craftsmanship, job completion, or failure to generally meet customer expectations."
2. Delivery-delay damage
3. Unsatisfactory repair
4. Credit/billing
5. Product quality
6. Guarantee/warranty
7. Failure to provide refunds
8. Selling practices
9. Advertising practices
10. Discontinued business

In order for you to determine what you want, you must determine as precisely as possible the nature of your complaint. Generally, it will fit within the list of the ten categories the Bureau has identified.

2. What impact has the problem had on you?

What the merchant doesn't realize is that when he fails to deliver what has been promised, you as the customer have to suffer the consequences.

To rectify the problem you'll have to spend time, money, and effort. Although the problem was not of your making, you are in a troubled situation that by all rights should not have occurred.

By pointing out the impact the problem had on you, you are showing cause and effect; you are showing that a failure on the merchant's part has created problems you need resolved—quickly.

Case history: I had a problem with improper billing. A company informed its attorneys to send a dunning letter to collect on a specific invoice; the attorneys dutifully sent a letter that smoked of fire and brimstone, with hints of imminent legal action.

The problem, of course, was that I had paid the bill a half year ago.

The cause: An error in the bookkeeping. *The effect:* A considerable effort on my part to prove I had already paid the bill. (I had to check through paid invoices, find the cancelled check, photocopy it, send copies to the attorneys, and send duplicate paperwork to the company that erroneously instructed their attorneys to come after me.

By showing the company was at fault and the consequences it had on me, it was obvious that this was a problem that required immediate rectification on their part.

The company instructed an executive to call and apologize to me, instructed the attorney to write and apologize, and then flew its people to see the attorneys to discuss how their collection letters should be written to get the point across without demeaning the customer.

3. What is your history as a customer with the merchant?

Because the merchant realizes that you are either a new customer or a regular customer, put yourself in perspective to his business.

If you are a new customer, you should stress that you are looking forward to a mutually satisfactory long-term relationship, that you patronize his store and expect to do so in the future, if your problem can be resolved.

If you are a regular customer, even if he doesn't know you by name or on sight, you represent ongoing business that you are sure the merchant would not like to lose.

Merchants need to be reminded that, ultimately, they work for you. If you aren't happy, then you'll take your business elsewhere. This simple but powerful argument puts every situation in perspective. In today's competitive climate, businesses must "recruit" new customers and, even more important, retain the ones they already serve.

4. Why does the problem exist?

By answering this question, you are showing that the merchant is accountable for the problem, not you. Of course, since the merchant created the problem, he is responsible for taking care of it for you. If you can show him who is responsible, it will be easier for him to take corrective action.

Case in point: In the incident where I was being dunned for a bill I had already paid, the problem existed because an error had been made on the part of the company's billing department. In addition, the offensive collection letters reflected poorly on the company and the attorneys they retained. By pointing out these two areas, management was able to get involved by setting up a system to minimize erroneous billings; in addition, they sent their people to see the attorneys, who had to rewrite the letters to be used in the future. (I might add that a year later, I had the same problem; I was dunned for a bill that had been paid. But at least the collection letter was civil and professional, which made all the difference in how I perceived the situation.)

5. Who do you feel is responsible for causing the problem?

By answering this question, you are holding someone accountable. Once you've determined *why* the problem exists, you can usually determine *who* or what department created the problem.

To correct the problem at its source, management will delegate the problem back down to the level where it originated; management can also check to insure the problem has been resolved.

It is very important to keep good records on who you talked or wrote to when addressing your complaint; promises will be made; but you must know *who* made the promises and be able to hold them to it later. In cases where you can't be specific in stating who you talked to, what was discussed and when, you are making it easy for a company to respond: "I'm sorry, but I don't know who would have told you that. It's against our policies, and I can't imagine they'd tell you something that's wrong."

Case in point: When a friend had a problem with a car dealership about unwanted insurance in connection with a new car purchase, he made sure he took notes on everything that was said, by whom, and when. As a result, it was clear that his position was correct and a refund check was immediately issued.

By not keeping records on promises made, everything can become confused and muddled because people can't be held accountable for their actions and what they say *unless* you can back up everything you claim by citing names, dates, subject discussed, and promises made.

6. What have you done to correct the problem?

By answering this question, you are showing that you have in good faith done everything you can possibly do. Therefore, what can the merchant do? After all, you've expended your best efforts; surely it's time for him to expend his.

You should discuss what actions you have taken: phone calls made, personal visits, letters written, and the results. You should show that no matter what you have done—and you've done everything possible from your end—nothing has worked; therefore, the merchant must in good faith reciprocate and meet you halfway; he must make a real effort to help resolve the problem. *What more can you do?*

7. What actions do you want taken to correct the problem?

This is the pivotal question: what do *you* want?

Before you answer, ask yourself some questions: What am I legally entitled to? (If you don't know, check with your attorney or with the Better Business Bureau.) What would be considered fair and reasonable on behalf of the merchant?

If what you are asking is unreasonable, you aren't going to get it. The point, of course, is that what you want should be an equitable solution for both you and the merchant. Remember, you are working toward a "win-win" situation, not a situation in which you get everything you want at the merchant's expense.

Case in point: A woman buys a new freezer but declines the extended warranty package; years after the regular warranty expires, the motor dies and the food spoils. She complains and wants a new refrigerator and reimbursement for the spoiled food. Will she get it? Chances are she won't.

Again, be reasonable in your demands. If you can't resolve your problem because you've made unreasonable demands on the merchant, chances are anyone else looking at your situation—arbitrators, mediators, or judges—will look at the merits of your case and determine that you were unrealistic in your expectations.

8. When do you expect a response?

Regardless of what they tell you, there's no excuse today for a merchant to drag out the situation by delaying action. It's in his best interests to look into the problem and get back to you as soon as possible; after all, he created the problem and, knowing that you are having to suffer the consequences, he should rectify it immediately.

State that you expect a response within two weeks; that's enough time for any business to look into the situation and get back with you, if you've provided them with all the specifics necessary to investigate the matter.

Any company that can't resolve a complaint quickly won't have your business for long. Don't accept excuses for why it takes so long to get a problem corrected; in truth, the excellent companies that *live* customer service know they can't affort to give excuses—and they don't.

Sample Complaint Letters

Obviously, it is not practical or possible to cover every complaint variation; most complaints will fall within one of the sample letters provided. Using the body of the letter as a model, you can write your own letter.

Keep in mind that the sample letters are suggestions only; change them as you wish to suit your particular needs.

The format of the letter

The sample letters provided offer suggestions on the body of the letter itself. The format of your letter should look the same, regardless of the kind of letter you are writing.

Center — the number of the certified mail receipt	Certified Letter #P 526 556 260
Your address	Mr. John Doe 3434 Main Street Anytown, VA 23666
The recipient's address	Mr. Attila B. Hun Hun Motor Company, Inc. Manager, Customer Relations 4302 Steppe Road Hampton, VA 23666
Subject of your letter	Re: Improper Billing on Invoice #2303
Salutation	Dear Mr. Hunn,
Body text of letter (paragraphs should all be flush left)	Start of first paragraph. Start of second paragraph. Start of third paragraph, etc.
Complimentary close	Sincerely Yours,
Your signature (make it legible!)	
Your name	Mr. John Doe
Indicates enclosure (or enclosures) to your letter	Enclosure

Letter 1, Unsatisfactory Service, Installation

Para-graph	Checklist	Example
	[ ] Re: _____	Re: Unsatisfactory service, installation
#1	[ ] date of delivery	5 January 1988
	[ ] product delivered	Miracle Heat Woodstove
	[ ] problem encountered	smoke filling room
	[ ] corrective action I took	hired chimney sweep to inspect and was charged $40
#2	[ ] relationship with company	long-standing
#3	[ ] problem	damper not removed
#4	[ ] costs involved	$40, paid on check # 302
#5	[ ] action requested	reimbursement of $40 for labor

Discussion

When the problem stems from an improper installation, the product may have to be removed, reinstalled, or corrective action taken to correct an actual deficiency like the example above.

Usually, the accountable persons are the installers, who answer to an installation supervisor.

Be sure to contact the company *immediately* after you've determined the installation to be substandard, since the installed product won't work as it should unless properly installed—a safety consideration.

Be sure to explain *why* the installation is substandard and what has to be done to correct it.

Letter 1:

Unsatisfactory Service

(Installation)

Letter to Installation Supervisor

Re: Unsatisfactory service (installation)

1. On 5 January 1988 your people delivered to my house for installation a Miracle Heat Woodstove. That night when we began burning wood in it, smoke began to fill back into the room. As a result, we called a chimney sweep who pulled the fireplace insert out of the fireplace and determined that the damper was not removed. The labor charge was $40.

2. As a long-standing customer with your firm, I'm surprised to see that your factory-trained servicemen could make such an error.

3. Had the damper been removed when it should have been during initial installation, there would have been no problem.

4. Because it was late at night and we needed the heat, we called the chimney sweep. His charge of $40 was paid by us on check #302.

5. Because the problem was due to improper installation, I am asking that you reimburse me $40 for the labor involved to correct the problem. I expect to hear from you within two weeks.

Sincerely Yours,

John A. Doe

Enclosure: Photocopy of the bill, invoice #0134

Letter 2, Unsatisfactory Service, Craftsmanship

Para graph	Checklist	Example
	Re: _____	Unsatisfactory service, craftsmanship
#1	[ ] date of delivery	6 October 1987
	[ ] product delivered	sofa
	[ ] amount paid	$565.45, check #404
	[ ] poor craftsmanship	staple-gun used to secure fabric
#2	[ ] relationship to store	new customer expressing concern
#3	[ ] accountable person	people who assembled the sofa
#4	[ ] what you've done	talked to Mr. Curtis Jackson, the salesman, who said to contact the customer service manager
#5	[ ] what you want	to have the sofa picked up, fixed, or replaced
	[ ] where you can be reached	by phone at work or home

Discussion

When the problem is poor craftsmanship, the product either has to be repaired or replaced. If it's a local product, a repair may be possible; if it's from a national manufacturer, which would involve shipping the product back, it's easier to get a replacement product.

Be sure to indicate precisely what you perceive as poor craftsmanship; be specific.

Letter 2:

Unsatisfactory Service

(Craftsmanship)

Letter to Customer Service Manager

Re: Unsatisfactory service (craftsmanship)

1. On 6 October 1987 your company delivered to me a new sofa that I had paid $565.45 on check #404. After inspecting the sofa carefully, I was surprised to discover that the craftsmanship of the sofa is shoddy: Staple-guns were used to secure fabric, which have already torn the fabric.

2. As a new customer I'm surprised to discover that you hadn't inspected the product carefully before delivery. I hope this is not typical, as I was given your name in recommendation from a good friend who spoke highly of your company.

3. Obviously, during the assembly of the sofa, your people cut a few corners to save time. It doesn't appear that the sofa can be easily repaired.

4. I have talked to your salesman, Mr. Curtis Jackson, who said he can't do anything about it. He did indicate that you are the customer service manager and could arrange for a replacement.

5. Please arrange to have this defective sofa picked up and have it fixed or, if necessary, be prepared to replace it. I look forward to hearing from you. I can be reached at (804) 402-2220 during business hours, or at home after 6:00 P.M. at (804) 332-3949.

Sincerely Yours,

Jane A. Doe

Enclosure: Invoice #402 (sales receipt)

Letter 3, Unsatisfactory Service, Job Completion

Para-graph	Checklist	Example
	Re: _____	Unsatisfactory service, job completion
#1	[ ] date delivered [ ] product [ ] purpose [ ] person accountable	6 January 1988 Kerosan heater, #504 tune-up Mr. Jimmy Jackson
#2	[ ] relationship to company	frequent customer
#3	[ ] problems on company's part	job was not completed because of heavy workload and improper supervision
#4	[ ] actions you had taken	made several phone calls, with no resolution
#5	[ ] action requested	look into this problem immediately

Discussion

When a job is not completed on time, it will create additional problems. In this case, because the Kerosan heater was not repaired when promised, the customer did without the supplemental heat during a cold snap.

Delays result when a company has taken on too much work and lacks the time or people to get the work done. Typically, you'll hear a lot of promises on when the work will be done; be sure to check up and hold people accountable.

The key here is to be persistent. Don't let them forget you need the job done—now! If you don't, someone else will pressure them. The squeaky wheel gets the grease.

Letter 3:

Unsatisfactory Service
(job completion)

Letter to Manager of Hardy Hardware

Re: Unsatisfactory service (job completion)

1. On 6 January 1988 I dropped off to your store a Kerosan heater, model number 504 for a tune-up. Because the cold snap was due to hit soon, I wanted to have the tune-up done immediately, which your salesman, Mr. Jimmy Jackson, said he would do that day.

2. As a frequent customer, I'm surprised to see that the repair work was not done on time. This is unusual for your company, even if the workload is heavy.

3. Because your salesman didn't finish the job as he had planned, I asked another salesman to help. Mr. John Simms said that the parts were on hand, but Jackson had them and he'd have to put them on. It turned out that after talking with Jackson on the phone, he said other work had come in that caused him to be late in working on the tune-up.

4. I made several phone calls to Jackson and to Simms on 7 January 1988 and 8 January 1988, but it seems impossible to get a straight answer.

5. Can you look into this and get the Kerosan heater fixed immediately? Please call me at work (830-4402) or at home after 6:00 P.M. at 830-3302 to inform me when my heater will be ready for pick-up.

Sincerely Yours,

Janet Florence

Letter 4, Unsatisfactory Service, Failure to meet expectations

Para-graph	Checklist	Example
	Re: _____	Unsatisfactory service, failure to meet expectations
#1	[ ] date of purchase [ ] product ordered [ ] the problem	6 January 1988 Supralite computer, model #403 difficult to read the screen
#2	[ ] problem with the manufacturer	can't adjust the screen to suit personal needs
#3	[ ] how you worked with the company to find alternatives	talked to the salesman, Rick Fisher, who showed the newer, more readable models
#4	[ ] action requested	have credit given toward an alter- nate computer, the Questar 1000
	[ ] where you can be reached	at home or at work

Discussion

Sometimes, no matter what you do, you'll buy a product, get it home, use it, and find out that it's unsuited for your needs. While the product isn't defective, it just isn't what you want.

Check with the salesman, then check with the store manager if necessary. Stress that you bought the product in good faith, but it's not meeting your expectations—in fact, you can't use it! Be sure to have alternatives to suggest: a replacement computer, an exchange for another computer, or a refund. In this case, product substitution or exchange is reasonable.

Letter 4:

Unsatisfactory Service

(failure to meet expectations)

Letter to Manager of Horizon Computer Store

Re: Unsatisfactory service (failure to meet expectations)

1. On 6 January 1988 I purchased a Supralite computer, model #403, that I bought for the purpose of taking it with me on airplane flights so I could write memos and letters, since I travel extensively and wanted to get maximum productivity out of my time. Unfortunately, the screen display is so light that, no matter what I do, it's hard to read.

2. I checked over the computer carefully, and it appears that the controls for darkening the screen can't be adjusted to suit my vision. Obviously, it's a personal problem of mine that I had not known existed with this model until I tried to use the computer on a recent plane flight.

3. I talked to the salesman, who said he couldn't exchange it without your permission. The salesman, Mr. Rick Fisher, showed me some of the newer models with different screen displays that seemed very easy to read.

4. With your permission I'd like to turn in the computer I bought and have credit given on a Questar 1000 computer, which has the gas plasma screen and is easy to read under any conditions. If this can be done, please call me at work or at home after 7:00 p.m. so that we can arrange for the exchange.

Sincerely Yours,

John Jackson

Enclosure: sales receipt

Letter 5, Delay in Delivery

Para-graph	Checklist	Example
	Re: _____	Delay in delivery
#1	[ ] product purchased	desk
	[ ] date purchased	10 March 1988
	[ ] promised delivery date	within two days
	[ ] product ordered	desk #403
	[ ] payment	$250 on check #403
#2	[ ] promise	delivery on the 11th
#3	[ ] problem	nondelivery
	[ ] action taken	called and talked to Mr. Jones, who promised delivery by the end of the day on the 12th
#4	[ ] store problem	promises of delivery from Mr. Jones, who hadn't delivered when promised
#5	[ ] action requested	the store will have to arrange a mutually agreeable time for delivery

Discussion

There's nothing more frustrating than ordering a product and not having it delivered, especially when you've taken off work or wasted a day waiting for a product that never arrives. Usually, the problem is an overcommitment in deliveries, which means everything is delayed; unfortunately, companies rarely notify you when they are going to be late.

Typically, a company cannot and will not give you an approximate delivery time beyond an "AM" or "PM" delivery. If you don't get your product on time, call immediately; they may have a CB radio or other means of contacting their deliveryman who is in the field.

Letter 5:

Delay in Delivery

Letter to Manager of Hinds Department Store

Re: Delay in delivery

1. On 10 March 1988 I was in your store and purchased a desk that was to be scheduled for delivery within two days. I bought a 60-inch office desk, product #403, for which I paid $250.00 on check #403. Unfortunately, the desk did not arrive and I am currently without a desk.

2. When I called the person who schedules your furniture delivery, Mr. Sammy Jones, he said that I'd have to be available all day, since he didn't know when his people could arrive on the 11th. By the end of the day, it was obvious that nobody was going to show up.

3. I called on the 12th, and Mr. Jones said that there was a late delivery and they couldn't get to my delivery. He promised me that he'd have the desk at my house by the end of the day.

4. I have made repeated phone calls to Mr. Jones, who keeps making promises that he can't deliver. I have taken off two days, waiting for a desk that has never arrived.

5. I can no longer wait for delivery during the day; please call me to arrange for a delivery after 6:00 p.m. Obviously, I can no longer stay home from work to suit your delivery schedule. After the problems I've had with delivery, you should suit your delivery schedule to mine. Call me at work or at home to arrange for a delivery schedule date and time.

Sincerely Yours,

Paul Garnett

Letter 6, Delivery Damage

Para-graph	Checklist		Example
	Re: _____		Damage in Delivery
#1	[ ]	date of delivery	16 March 1988
	[ ]	product being delivered	a 19-inch Songsung TV
	[ ]	who delivered	Mr. Frank Jackson
	[ ]	problem noted	dents in the TV cabinet
#2	[ ]	relationship to the company	long-standing customer
#3	[ ]	cause of damage	mishandling from the warehouse to the house
#4	[ ]	company contact and problem	talked to salesman, who said it had been signed for "in good condition," so there's nothing that he can do
#5	[ ]	what you want	defective cabinet exchanged for a new one

Discussion

Regardless of whether the product you order arrives through the mail, United Parcel Service (UPS), or local delivery, if the product is damaged during shipping, the shipper can be liable, unless it's obvious that improper packaging was contributory.

In the case of local deliveries, mishandling of the product can cause damage. Unfortunately, you may sign for the product in good faith and realize, after the fact, that it was damaged in transit—a problem you didn't create.

Be sure to check out the product *when you take the delivery* and make the deliveryman aware of any problems with damage. Be sure you know who you talked to, and when. Then follow-up with a phone call or letter to his immediate supervisor, who can make arrangements to replace or exchange the defective product.

Don't procrastinate; the longer you wait, the more it will appear that you might have caused the damage yourself. Act promptly when you have this problem, or the company may honestly feel they didn't damage the product in transit.

Letter 6:

Delivery Damage

Letter to Customer Service Manager

Re: Damage in Delivery

1. On 16 March 1988 your delivery man, Mr. Frank Jackson, came to my house to deliver a 19-inch Songsung television. After he brought the TV into the living room, I noticed that the wood cabinet had been dented. Unfortunately, because the scars are in the back, I didn't notice them until after I had signed for the TV.

2. I've been a customer at your store for a long time. One of the reasons I shop there is because you've always put the customer first, even if it means giving him the benefit of the doubt.

3. Doubtless the damage occurred during transportation of the TV from your warehouse to my house; I imagine the cabinet of the TV was accidentally nicked against a door frame as it was brought into the house.

4. I talked to the salesman, who said he couldn't do anything after the TV had been signed for by me, indicating that I had received it in good condition. Obviously, there's nothing more I can do.

5. Can you arrange to have the defective cabinet exchanged for a new one? Your delivery people can schedule a mutually convenient time to make the exchange, if they'll call me at work or at home after 6:00 p.m. I look forward to hearing from you within the week.

Sincerely Yours,

George Wilson

Enclosure: Receipt of delivery form

Letter 7, Unsatisfactory Repair

Para-graph	Checklist	Example
	Re: _____	Unsatisfactory repair
#1	[ ] the date the product was turned over to the company	6 March 1988
	[ ] product	Izawa, two-door sports coupe
	[ ] diagnosis	worn brake linings
	[ ] problem	one brake lining still worn
#2	[ ] independent verification by competent authority	Mr. Bob Jones, a mechanic, test-drove the car and found a problem
#3	[ ] problem	faulty work on the company's part, requiring $30 labor to inspect the car independently
	[ ] what you want	to have the car repaired and reimbursement for the independent inspection costing $30
#4	[ ] what you want done	a phone call to discuss a time to have the car dropped off for immediate repairs

Discussion

Poor repair work is a major problem, especially with complex products like automobiles. It's important to get estimates in writing so you aren't overcharged, and if the estimate goes over because of parts or labor overruns, you should be notified immediately, appraised of the situation, and be able to make a determination if you want to pay the extra charges.

If the repair work was not done, resulting in the same problems recurring, or if the repair work creates new problems, take the product back and get them to work on it again, at their expense. (For example, if your car starts poorly and, after it's been worked on, the car still starts poorly, they haven't done the job right—but you've been charged. They should fix the problem free because you've already paid once for what should have been corrected the *first* time.)

If the repair problem is obviously an omission on their part, they should repair and replace for free.

If you feel the repair work was not done right, have it independently verified by another repairman; this way, you've got a strong case of possible negligence on the part of the company.

Letter 7:

Unsatisfactory Repair

Letter to the Manager of the automotive repair shop

> *Re: Unsatisfactory Repair*
>
> 1. On 6 March 1988 I left with your people my 1986 Izawa, two-door sports coupe, which you diagnosed as having worn brake linings. Unfortunately, when I got the car back on 8 March, it sounded as if one brake lining was still worn.
>
> 2. When I took the car to a nearby service station, the mechanic, Mr. Bob Jones, took the car for a drive and then told me that he'd have to look at the two rear wheels. When he took the left rear wheel off, he showed me where new brake pads were not mounted, resulting in wear against the rotor.
>
> 3. I will be dropping my car off to your service facility tomorrow. I expect you to install new brake pads on the left rear wheel and also reimburse me the $30 for labor incurred when the other mechanic had to inspect the wheel to determine the problem. Obviously, if your people had double-checked the work, they would have found an extra set of brake pads on hand or noticed the error during a test-drive, which I'm told was not done.
>
> 4. Call me tomorrow to arrange for a mutually convenient time for me to drop off the car to your shop for immediate repairs.
>
> Sincerely,
>
>
> Lucy Jackson
> Enclosure: Bill of $30 from Acme Service Station

Letter 8, Credit/Billing Error

Para-graph	Checklist	Example
	Re: _____	Billing error
#1	[ ] date payment made	5 September 1987
	[ ] amount of payment	$225
	[ ] your account number	#3030
	[ ] place payment made	branch office at Mid-Center Plaza
	[ ] problem	payment not posted
#2	[ ] continued problems	late notices and phone calls from the credit department
#3	[ ] company's error	wrong posting to another account with similar name
	[ ] company's promise	check-up to insure delinquent credit not filed on credit reports
#4	[ ] action requested	Check to insure that the erroneous, negative information was not sent to the credit bureaus

Discussion

With the advent of computerized billing, customer service departments have found it too easy to say "it's the computer's fault." The truth is that the computer carries out instructions it's been programmed to do by a person—someone in the company is responsible, not the computer!

Billing problems are difficult to resolve quickly because one error leads to the next, resulting in a flood of phone calls, reminders, and late notices that are difficult to stop. In some cases, especially where payments are to be made, customer service people simply have been burned too frequently by people with hard-luck stories and excuses that they don't give you with the legitimate complaint the attention you deserve.

In cases where it's obvious that you are getting jerked around, ask to speak to the supervisor. Typically, account representatives are difficult to reach on the phone and at times even refuse to tell you who they are.

Make sure you keep careful records of any phone calls and correspondence or billings you've received; you are going to have to prove you weren't at error, and documentation is the way you will prove your point.

Letter 8:

Credit/Billing Error

Letter to Customer Service

> *Re: Billing Error*
>
> 1. On 5 September 1987 I made a car payment of $225 on my account #3030 at the branch office in the Mid-Center Plaza. One week later, I received a late notice from your credit department, indicating that the payment hadn't been made, and could I please contact their department?
>
> 2. Obviously, I had made the payment, but for some reason it has not been credited to my account. In the interim, I've received another late notice reminder and a phone call from your credit department.
>
> 3. After talking with your credit department, it appears that the money was posted to another account, to an individual with a similar name. I'm not entirely sure my account has been cleared, though I've been told it has been "cleaned" of any delinquency notices.
>
> 4. Can you check to insure my payment history is clean and that negative information was not forwarded to the credit bureaus? Please call me this week at your convenience to inform me of your findings.
>
> Best,
>
>
> Michael Smith
>
> Enclosure: Bank receipt for car payment

Letter 9, Product Quality

Discussion

Product quality is a sticky issue because how you perceive it as the customer and how the company perceives it can be worlds apart. What they view as a satisfactory product may strike you as poor in quality.

To protect yourself *before* you buy, know what the store's policy is on exchanges and refunds. If the product is damaged or defective, you may have a difficult time getting an exchange locally unless the store policy is liberal. If necessary to get satisfaction, you may have to write to the corporate office and explain the situation to the customer service department, or possibly to the president of the company.

Be sure you can substantiate what you claim; be specific in your objection to the product, so it won't appear that you are simply dissatisfied on general grounds, which will reflect unfavorably on you.

Product Quality

Letter to President of Hot-Stuff Coffee Machines, Inc.

Re: Product quality

1. I recently bought one of your Hot Stuff Coffee Machines, which you are promoting heavily as the best coffee machines available in the marketplace. Unfortunately, the one I bought, product #450, is not of high quality; in fact, I feel the quality is substandard when compared to other machines I have owned.

2. I've bought many of your products over the years and am quite surprised that your new Hot Stuff Coffee Machine, product #450, leaks coffee because of its "new design spout." The problem is obviously a design problem; exchanging my coffee machine for a new one would not solve the problem.

3. I spoke with the store manager about the coffee machine, and he indicated that since it's not a structural defect, he can't make an adjustment. I would like your customer service department or local store manager to issue me a refund in full of $39.95 when the machine is returned to the place of your convenience.

4. Please contact me within two weeks as I'd like to get another machine to replace the defective one with another model or another brand.

Sincerely yours,

Cuyler W. Warnell

Enclosure: sales receipt
                photocopy of cancelled check #302, $39.95

Letter 10, Guarantee/Warranty

Para-graph	Checklist	Example
	Re: _____	Guarantee/Warranty
#1	[ ] date product purchased	5 January 1987
	[ ] salesman	Mr. Bob Jones
	[ ] warranty	one-year
	[ ] paperwork	warranty paperwork filled out by Jones and mailed in from store
#2	[ ] problem	warranty work needed
#3	[ ] continued problems with the company	despite warranty, store does not honor warranty work
#4	[ ] your efforts	phone calls and two trips to the store
#5	[ ] what you want	repaired machine immediately

Discussion

A frequent problem with guarantee warranty claims is that the customer does not have the paperwork necessary to document the case. You'll have to show proof of purchase with the original sales slip and invoice, and proof that you mailed the warranty paperwork in. Without the warranty paperwork on hand at corporate headquarters, you won't get warranty work done at the manufacturer's expense.

Be persistent in getting what you paid for; warranties are specific in what they cover—but not necessarily what they don't If you have any questions about warranty coverage, ask *before you buy.*

Because the local dealer is reimbursed for any warranty work he does, he will want to make sure that he's covered by checking to see that corporate headquarters had received your original paperwork; he will check before beginning work.

Letter 10:

Guarantee/Warranty

Letter to Customer Service, corporate level

Re: Warranty

1. On 5 January 1987 I bought from Mr. Bob Jones a Master Lawn Mower with leaf bag that came with a one-year warranty. The paperwork for the warranty was filled out at the store and mailed in by Mr. Jones.

2. In December of the same year, just before the warranty expired, I took in the mower for warranty work because it was very difficult to start. Mr. Jones indicated that it would need a slight adjustment.

3. Having taken the mower to him twice for a "slight adjustment" and finding out that the electric starter still doesn't work, I asked him to replace the mower, since your warranty promised to "fix or replace at our option any defective part or product."

4. I have made repeated phone calls (see phone log attached) and two visits to get the lawn mower fixed, but it is still defective. Please have another service center pick up this mower to determine why it won't start and, if necessary, replace the machine immediately as I'm unable to cut grass until it is fixed. I look forward to hearing from you within the week.

Sincerely,

John Jones,

Enclosures: phone log
        warranty paperwork

Letter 11, Failure to provide refunds

Para-graph	Checklist	Example
		Failure to provide refunds
	Re: _____	
#1	[ ] date of purchase	6 March 1987
	[ ] product purchased	Ice Cream Machine model #502
	[ ] purchased from	Ms. Debra Hines at the department store in Hampton, VA
#2	[ ] accountable person	Mrs. Cecille Sentara, who promised to see that the refund check was mailed
#3	[ ] what you want	Have the customer service manager look into this and get back to you immediately

Discussion

In cases where a refund is due, you must be persistent. Be sure you have the original sales receipt and know the store's refund policies. (Some stores will repair or replace at their option, others will exchange freely, and yet others will issue credit only for other merchandise.)

If you don't get the refund quickly, then work within the chain of command of the company, going to the corporate customer service department and, if necessary, to the president, who will delegate this to one of his assistants.

Don't let them forget you; keep calling and writing until you get the refund you've been promised.

Letter 11:

Failure to Provide Refunds

Letter to president of company

Re: Failure to Provide Refund

1. On 6 March 1987 I purchased an Ice Cream Machine, model #502, from Ms. Debra Hines at your department store in Hampton, Virginia. Although the product worked well for the first month, it broke down in the second month.

2. I contacted your corporate customer service department, which took the product back and promised to mail me a refund within a week. The woman whom I spoke to initially, Mrs. Cecille Sentara, said that if the check didn't arrive in a week, I should call her. I then called, and she said she thought it had been mailed, and that she'd get back to me.

3. To date she has not gotten back to me. Can you please have your customer service manager look into this and get back to me within the week? I'd like to know why I haven't gotten the refund yet, and when I can expect to have the refund mailed.

Sincerely yours,

Bob C. Ratchett

Enclosure: Sales receipt

Letter 12, Selling Practices Complaint

Para-graph	Checklist	Example
	Re: _____	Selling practices complaint
#1	[ ] date of the incident [ ] location [ ] salesman [ ] subject under discussion	5 February 1988 car dealership on Main Street Mr. Jesse Barrett financing
#2	[ ] problem	Salesperson pushing on-the-spot financing too aggressively
#3	[ ] your perception	a pressure tactic to get you to use the dealer financing instead of credit union financing
#4	[ ] what you want	another salesman to represent the sale

Discussion

We've all had the experience of buying from a salesperson whose eye was on the immediate commission and not on our needs. In cases where the salesperson is obviously trying to manipulate you—using high pressure sales tactics to get you to buy immediately, to buy what he wants you to buy, or to "take" his recommendations without consideration—be quick to change salespeople or, if necessary, go to another dealer.

In cases where the selling practices are suspect and disregard for the customer is rampant throughout the local company, bring it to the attention of the store manager or, if necessary, to the president of the company at corporate level.

Don't let the salesperson intimidate you by using deceptive selling techniques and misinformation to get you to do what he wants. Get another one—and complain!

Letter 12:

Selling Practices Complaint

Letter to Store Owner

Re: Complaint about Selling Practices

1. On 5 February 1988 I was in the showroom of your car dealership located on Main Street when I got into a discussion with one of your salesmen, Mr. Jesse Barrett, about my preference in having my credit union finance the car instead of having it financed on the premises through a local bank.

2. My problem is that Mr. Barrett, in his interest in closing the sale immediately, spoke poorly of the credit union of which I'm a member, saying that "credit there is easier to get than at a bank," indicating that my "credit history would look stronger if it showed bank financing."

3. I'm not sure if the salesman was speaking in ignorance, or whether he was trying to meet his monthly quota, but the information he gave me was incorrect and, worse, struck me as a pressure tactic to get me to finance through one of his preferred sources instead of having it financed myself.

4. Please have another salesperson contact me because I'd like to buy the car, but I don't feel comfortable with that particular one making the sale.

Sincerely,

Frank Kelly

Letter 13, Advertising Practices

Para- graph	Checklist	Example
	Re: _____	Advertising Practices
#1	[ ] misleading ad appearance	morning edition of Hampton *Herald*
	[ ] product advertised	VHS-format videocassette recorder with wireless remote for $230.95
	[ ] problem	In the store, the wireless remote control was $45 additional
#2	[ ] deceptive ad	ad showed a wireless remote at the price of $230.95; no mention of sur- charge for the wireless remote
#3	[ ] what you want	To have the price honored as advertised for the product depicted
#4	[ ] your expectation	To get a phone call confirming a VHS-format recorder will be held for you at the advertised price

Discussion

Ads can be deceptive—the product advertised may not be an exact representation of what you are buying; the product may be advertised at a base price, with tiny print to indicate that "the computer monitor is optional," as if you can use a computer without it; or the ad could be cleverly worded to catch your attention, although it is accurate but misleading.

Write a complaint letter to the local store and to the president of the company. Contact the local Better Business Bureau, which promotes truth in advertising and will look into any deceptive advertising on the behalf of all consumers.

Letter 13:

Advertising Practices

Letter to Store Manager

Re: Advertising Practices

1. In the morning edition of the Hampton *Herald,* you advertised a VHS-format videocassette recorder with wireless remote for $230.95 plus tax. When I went to the store to buy it, you pointed out that the VHS with wired remote was $230.95, and that the wireless remote model was extra: $45 more!

2. The ad you published in the newspaper clearly showed a wireless remote at the price of $230.95 At no time did it indicate that there would be a higher price for the wireless model.

3. I don't know whether the error is yours or in the department that prepares the ad for publication, but it is your responsibility to proof-read your ad to insure accuracy and proper pictorial content. I expect you to honor my order for the VHS-format recorder with wireless remote at the price quoted for the model shown in the newspaper ad.

4. Please call me this week to indicate one of the VHS-format recorders with wireless remote is being held for me at your Hampton store for the advertised price of $230.95 plus tax.

Sincerely,

Ira Leaven

Enclosure: Photocopy of Hampton *Herald* ad, 2/5/88

Letter 14, Discontinued Business

Para-graph	Checklist	Example
	Re: _____	Discontinued business
#1	[ ] date the problem arose	5 March 1988
	[ ] problem	withholding the security deposit, $400
	[ ] company claim	the deposit is owed to you, but from the previous company
#2	[ ] everything in a relative light	you can't afford the $400 loss, and you've been a good tenant; you've done nothing to warrant this treatment
#3	[ ] rights & obligations	you collect rent, you must also be liable for liabilities
#4	[ ] your efforts with the company	you spoke with the resident manager, Jack Shadwell, and the customer service people at 850-0221, who refused to help
#5	[ ] action desired	you want a $400 refund within the week

Discussion

In cases where the company has gone bankrupt, you have little recourse since its assets are going to be attached by creditors, who don't expect to get what they are owed; typically, they'll get a few cents on the dollar. In cases where a company has been bought out by another company, it is absorbing its assets and, reasonably, its liabilities. In that case, you can pursue your case.

In the situation I've described, a friend almost gave up in trying to get the deposit back. She then wrote a letter, explaining the situation, and after waiting a few weeks filed in small claims court. Once the company was served papers to appear in court, the refund check suddenly arrived.

If you don't know what your rights are in such matters, ask the Better Business Bureau to mediate. Or, if necessary, be prepared to file in small claims court.

Letter 14:

Discontinued Business

Letter to president of new company which bought out the old company

Re: Discontinued Business

1. On 5 March 1988 I spoke with your credit department, which said that the $400 security deposit I put down on my apartment a year ago would not be refunded by your company because you don't owe it; the former company owed it to me, and they are out of business.

2. The $400 represents a considerable sum of money that I can't afford to lose due to misunderstandings on rights and obligations of the former owner and current tenants, myself included. I've been at this apartment for a little under a year, during which time I've always paid my rent on time and kept the apartment in good condition.

3. As you now collect rent, it seems likely that you also are responsible for paying any security deposits; when you bought the company out, I must assume you acquired its assets and liabilities, in which case you owe me $400.

4. I have talked repeatedly to the resident manager, Mr. Jack Shadwell, and your customer service personnel at 850-0221, who refuse to help me in this matter.

5. I would like a check of $400 to be mailed to me within the week, which would then properly close the account.

Sincerely yours,

Frank Whitcomb

Enclosure: cancelled check #302, dated 5 March 1987, security deposit

Unfortunately, even the most reputable of companies will sometimes take the position that they are right and you are wrong, even if they legally are in error. In cases where you know what your rights are and pursue them through writing a complaint letter backed up with legal action, you'll find yourself being taken seriously; they can't ignore you.

Some companies take the notion that if they ignore you, you'll be a nice customer and go away. Don't *you* be the one to let them think like that; let them know that you only want what you've got coming to you—and you'll get it.

When Things Go Right

When things go right, write!

Robert Townsend, author of *Up the Organization*, remarked that thanks are a neglected form of compensation. So true!

When you receive outstanding service, take the time to use a comment card or write a letter to the President of the company. When an employee has gone out of his way to make your day, make his by letting his boss know how much you appreciate it.

Case in point: During a recent business trip to Anaheim, California, I stayed at the Hyatt Regency Alicante. Although the entire staff struck me as professional and helpful, nobody stood out—except the concierge. When he found out that one of his co-workers had lost my reservations for an airport limousine, he got on the phone, made reservations, calmed me down, and made sure I would make my flight. As I waited for the limo, flustered and anxious, the concierge reassured me every half hour until it arrived.

Upon returning to Virginia, I used a comment card, cited the concierge by name, and made sure the President knew how I felt.

Go ahead—make someone else's day.

Chapter **6**

The Better Business Bureau and You

Chances are good that when you think of the Better Business Bureau, commonly referred to as the Bureau, you think of them as a source of handling complaints. Unless you've dealt with them before, chances are good that you don't realize that they provide *preventive* information about local and national companies.

In 1986 the Bureau handled nearly 10 million inquiries and complaints. Of these, over 7 million were inquiries from potential customers wanting information before they buy; over 2 million were complaints. Clearly, today's consumer wants information *before* he buys—a position the Bureau and most consumer groups advocate.

Through its branch offices, the Bureau offers you help in two areas; preventive measures and complaint handling. Funded by dues paid by local businesses, the services provided are free.

Preventive Measures

As a source of information on local and national merchants, the Bureau provides reliability reports on local, regional, and national merchants. With these reports you will learn if a company has a satisfactory or unsatisfactory business performance rating. A satisfactory rating means that the business has satisfied all complaints brought against it, or never had any complaints filed. An unsatisfactory rating, however, can result from a number of reasons:

1. Not answering complaints filed by the Bureau.
2. Not settling complaints.
3. Not eliminating causes of complaints.
4. Using questionable selling practices.
5. Refusing to eliminate misleading or deceptive advertising practices.

In 1986 over 60 percent of all inquiry calls resulted in a company report being read or sent to the consumer. Obviously, a company with a poor record at the Bureau is a company that does not deserve your support. Chances are good that if the Bureau has a number of complaints, there are also scores of complaints that simply have never been filed; the customers, unhappy and frustrated, just leave and go to another store.

In addition, the Bureau maintains an information bank with pamphlets on over 100 areas of consumer interest. Although some may be available locally, all are available through the Bureau's main office in New York; a self-addressed, stamped envelope will bring you a list of the pamphlets available, which cost $1 each when ordered by mail.

Pamphlets available

"Advance Fee" Loans
Advertising Code
Advertising, Consumer Credit
Advertising & Home Financing
Air Conditioning, Central
Alarm Systems, Residential
American Economic System
Apartment Renting
Appliance Service
Arbitration Program, BBB
Autoline, BBB
Automatic Transmissions
Automobile, Advertising Offers
Automobile, Buying a New
Automobile, Buying a Used
Automobile, Car on the Road
Automobile, Renting
Automobile, Repair
Bait & Switch Tactics
Basement Waterproofing
Beauty Pageants
Better Business Bureau, Role of
Business Credit, Obtaining
Buying Clubs
Buying on Time
Cable TV
Carpets and Rugs
Charity Pleas
Computers, Home
Consumer Credit
Consumer Information
Contact Lenses
Contest Cons
Cosigning a Loan
Credit Billing
Credit Card Fraud
Customer Relations & Complaints
Door to Door Sales
Drycleaning
Elderly, Consumer Problems

Pest Control
Philanthropic Advisory Service
Phone, Buying a
Phone, Buying by
Phone, Investing by
Phony Invoices
Poison Prevention
Refunds, Exchanges & Returns
Sales Contracts
Savings & Investing
Schemes Against Business
Solar Energy for Your Home
Swimming Pools
Tires
Travel Packages
Utility Rate & Auditing Companies
Vacation Timesharing
Vending Machines, Automatic
Video Systems, Home
Water Conditioners
Women & Credit Histories
Work-at-Home Schemes

Complaint Handling

Best known for its complaint handling, the Bureau has a settlement index of 76.5 percent. The figure is high because businesses want to maintain a good record at the Bureau and, when approached with a legitimate complaint, will work with you to help resolve it, especially if the Bureau is involved in mediation or arbitration.

The Complaint-Handling Process

The Bureau recommends the following procedures in handling a complaint through them.

First, try to resolve your complaint directly with the merchant. Because most businesses realize your satisfaction is important for repeat business and referrals, they will try to satisfy you, so long as your demands are reasonable.

Second, if for whatever reasons you can't get your problem corrected by dealing direct, then call your local Bureau office and talk to a service representative, who after listening to your side of the story, will counsel you on what to do next.

93

Third, if the Bureau feels you have a legitimate complaint, write a cover letter to the Bureau with the complaint letter you mailed to the merchant.

Fourth, once they receive and review your letter, a copy is sent to the business.

This process, known as mediation, is the Bureau's attempt to bring about reconciliation through bringing the two parties together in an informal process. Acting as an impartial third party, the Bureau depends on a sense of fair play between you and the merchant.

If mediation fails, the next step is arbitration.

Arbitration

Though normally used to resolve big ticket disputes, usually car repair bills or construction bills, arbitration can be used to resolve virtually any consumer dispute.

Explained in its simplest terms, arbitration is a legally binding process in which a third person makes a decision involving a dispute. An alternative to legal action through the courts, arbitration operates on the basis that, depending on the issue, simple mediation is not enough; a decision by an impartial third person is necessary to act as judge, weigh the facts, and make a determination.

The Bureau's arbitration program follows the mediation process, which presents to the business the customer's complaint and seeks to get a response. When mediation fails, arbitration is the next step.

The steps involved:

1. You, the customer, sign an agreement with the business with whom you have a complaint; the agreement describes the specifics being disputed.

2. An arbitrator is chosen. Both you and the business select a volunteer from the local community, drawn from a list of five suggested names. If a conflict of interest exists, you cross that person off; the biography provided may reveal background information that could reveal the arbitrator as biased. Once ranked, the highest overlapping ranking is the arbitrator selected.

3. An informal hearing is presented at which you can represent yourself, bring an attorney, bring witnesses, then state your case.

The Bureau recommends you be prepared to prove your position is the right one, just as you would do in court. Bring all necessary paperwork—sufficient for copies to everyone involved—and indicate your witnesses. Then list in chronological order the steps you took to resolve the complaint. These steps should include (a) contacting the company directly by phone, (b) sending a complaint letter, preferably by registered mail, return receipt requested; and (c) sending the letter to the corporate office, if necessary.

Expect the company to defend itself and its position, using paperwork, witnesses, warranties/guarantees, and the steps they took to help you.

4. After both sides are heard, the arbitrator makes a decision, limited to the original issues as stated in the arbitration agreement you and the company have signed. There are four possible outcomes: (1) One or more parties may be required to act, (2) money must be paid, (3) the customer's claim can be rejected completely, or (4) the decision may be split, favoring the customer and the company, depending on the specifics of the claim.

Limitations of Arbitration

Though arbitration is legally binding, not all issues can be resolved through arbitration. Consequential damages, personal injury and property damage claims, fraud allegations, or other criminal law violations are not within the scope of arbitration; these require the services of an attorney who can represent you in court.

In addition, arbitration depends on an individual's determination of what is fair in the specifics of this case. Legal matters usually rely on precedent, prior cases, and rules of law that, when considered, can determine a different outcome than an arbitrated case. When in doubt, check with an attorney to see if legal recourse or Bureau arbitration is preferable.

Arbitration pamphlet available

The Bureau provides a free pamphlet on arbitration, "Arbitration: A National Program of Dispute Resolution, the Common Sense Alternative." This is available through the Bureau; ask for publication 24-165.

What the Bureau Can't Do

Because the Bureau promotes better business pactices through consumer education, mediation and arbitration, the Bureau works in a spirit of cooperation as an impartial third party between you and the company you are having problems with. The Bureau does have specific limitations:

1. The Bureau has no legal powers. It can't close down a business, give legal advice, or assist in breaching or voiding contracts made without fraud or misrepresentation.

2. It can't give out credit information.

3. It can't make collections.

4. It can't assist in labor disputes.

5. It makes no recommendations or endorsements.

6. It does not appraise articles or quality of services rendered.

In these cases, the Bureau may recommend where to go for additional help.

In researching this book, I spoke with an operations director at a local Bureau, who suggested I pass on some key points:

1. Prevention of problems through consumer education is the key to being a satisfied customer.

2. *Always let the company have a chance to resolve the problem.* If you don't give them the chance first, how do you know they won't help you?

3. When you complain to a company, your goal should be to bring your problem to the attention of the person who has the power to help you.

4. Be sure to get names of people you speak with when complaining to a company. Accountability is important if you expect to hold a company to its promises.

5. When dealing with small companies, remember that they may not be experienced in handling complaints because they may not know what their rights and obligations are. Though large companies usually have complaint departments, small ones may not, in which case they usually call the Bureau for advice.

6. Remember that the local Bureau receives hundreds of phone calls a day. Keep yours short and to-the-point when describing your problem.

7. Don't write to a company and carbon copy the Bureau. The Bureau will not act on your behalf, though they will acknowledge receiving the letter.

8. The Bureau generally does not handle on your behalf what they would consider an unjustified complaint. For instance, if you sign a contract to buy a car, then find a better deal down the street and want to break your contract but can't, the Bureau will not be able to help.

9. The Bureau does not take sides. They are impartial third parties only.

10. The Bureau will generally not handle cases where the company is 100 percent legally correct and you want to get your way.

11. Be polite when dealing with companies. Communications problems, misunderstandings and false expectations can be as much your problem as the company's.

Chapter 7

Mail Order

In 1984 consumers spent more than $54 billion on mail order merchandise from over 6,000 companies. In the same year, the Better Business Bureau reported in its annual statistical summary that "ordered product sales" ranked first in the top ten categories of complaint.

Before you buy anything by mail, consider the advantages, disadvantages, and know what your rights are when things go wrong.

Advantages

1. *Mail order is convenient.* No longer a tedious and time-consuming process of sending a check with the order, you can use your credit card and toll-free 800 number provided by the mail order company to order whatever you wish. If you are in a hurry, two-day United Parcel Service (UPS), overnight UPS, or overnight air couriers like Federal Express and DHL can practically guarantee delivery if you wish to pay the premium price.

2. *Mail order offers a diverse selection.* Though large metropolitan areas have department stores and specialized shops that cater to many tastes and whims, smaller communities may lack the diversity of products and services available. As we become consumers with increasingly specialized interests, mail order catalogs offer a way to order exactly what you want, when you want it.

3. *Mail order lets you shop at your pace.* You don't shop in haste, pressured by a salesperson on the floor, promoting the latest product he's got in stock. You shop at your leisure, at your own pace, without the pressure of salespeople trying to "close the sale."

4. *Mail order can save you money.* Because you are buying direct, you eliminate the middleman, the retailer who has overhead and must charge retail to cover the additional expense.

Depending on the company, service after the sale with a mail order firm can vary considerably. The best companies like Lands End, Zone VI, and L. L. Bean offer unconditional guarantees; other companies may not.

The question you should ask yourself: Is the initial savings enough to justify *not* having local retailer support in case you have a problem? (The more complex or mechanical your product, the more it makes sense to buy it locally and, if you have a problem, take it back to the dealer and let him handle it.)

Disadvantages

1. *Unordered merchandise is a hassle.* If you get shipped the wrong product, it takes time and a lot of paperwork to make the adjustment, return the unordered product, then have the new product shipped out. If

you are in a hurry, this can be a real problem.

2. *Merchandise may be out of stock.* Depending on what you buy and the time of year, the product you want may be out of stock. Of course, it's then back-ordered, but that doesn't do you any good if you need it now.

3. *Late delivery can make a difference.* Though there are Federal Trade Commission regulations on when products must be shipped, delays can result and you may be waiting for a product you need—today.

4. *Product may be damaged in delivery.* Product can be damaged in shipping, regardless of who shipped it and how it was packed.

5. *Repair work may be difficult.* The more complicated the product, the more it makes sense to buy it locally if the retailer can provide service after the sale. (I know a friend who ordered a computer by mail order; when it went down, he had to rent another computer instead of getting a loaner from a local store to carry him through until the repairs were done.)

In some cases, you may have to send the product back to the manufacturer to get it serviced. Then there's no guarantee it'll arrive back in working order, which means another round of shipping and waiting before you get your product back.

6. *General dissatisfactions can arise.* In some cases, you don't see what you are buying until you get it. What looks good or sounds promising in the catalog or ad may appear less desirable when you get the product and see it for the first time. Unlike a retail store where you can pick up the product, feel it, see it, and get a "hands on" orientation, the mail order product is in most cases ordered on the strength of what you see in print. What you expect and what you get may be worlds apart.

Minimizing Problems in Mail Order

Problems are inevitable, but you can prevent a lot of problems when ordering by mail by taking some common sense precautions.

1. *Deal only with reputable firms.* If you have not dealt with the company before, check it out. If it is new, it might not have any record on hand at the Better Business Bureau; however, if it has been around for a few years, it has an established track record.

2. *What are its policies on warranties, refunds, exchanges, repairs, and shipping problems?*

3. *Keep records of what you order.* When paying, use your credit card or check, which gives you a record of what you've bought; obviously, you should never send in cash because it can be lost in the mail and you've got no proof of purchase. Be sure you keep a record of what you order. If you have a typewriter, use it if your handwriting is difficult to read. (Some shipping problems result from not writing down your complete address

or, in some cases, writing illegibly.)

Photocopy the ad you've ordered from, the order form you used, any correspondence to the company, and record payment information in case you have to follow up with a claim.

Sample Letter

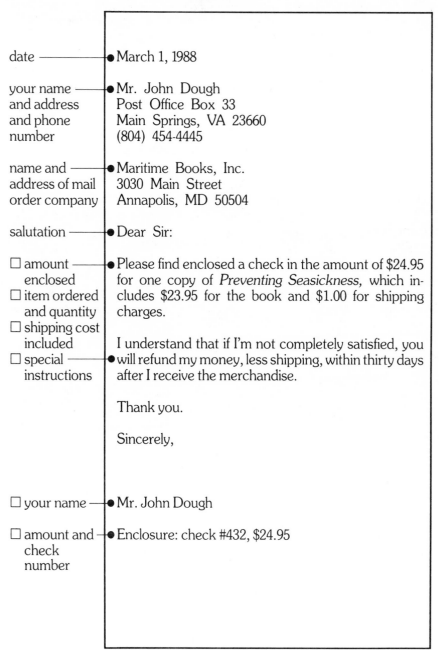

date	March 1, 1988
your name and address and phone number	Mr. John Dough Post Office Box 33 Main Springs, VA 23660 (804) 454-4445
name and address of mail order company	Maritime Books, Inc. 3030 Main Street Annapolis, MD 50504
salutation	Dear Sir:
☐ amount enclosed ☐ item ordered and quantity ☐ shipping cost included ☐ special instructions	Please find enclosed a check in the amount of $24.95 for one copy of *Preventing Seasickness,* which includes $23.95 for the book and $1.00 for shipping charges. I understand that if I'm not completely satisfied, you will refund my money, less shipping, within thirty days after I receive the merchandise. Thank you. Sincerely,
☐ your name	Mr. John Dough
☐ amount and check number	Enclosure: check #432, $24.95

101

Dealing with Problems in Mail Order

1. *Unsolicited mail.* If you are deluged with "junk" mail, write to DMA (Direct Marketing Association) for a standard form that will remove your name from mailing lists.

Whenever you buy anything, you get on that company's mailing list and, if they sell your name to a mailing list broker, you'll find yourself on other lists, too. You can minimize this by stating on your order form or original letter that you do not wish to have your name sold to any other company for mail list purposes.

2. *Unsatisfactory product.* Before you buy, find out what the policies are for exchanges, replacements, repair work, lost merchandise, warranty work, etc. *Don't wait until after you have a problem to complain.*

3. *Damaged goods.* If the package arrives by the Postal Service and if it's obvious that damage has been done to the package, mark it "REFUSED, RETURN TO SENDER" *at the time of delivery.* It will be sent back, unless you've signed for the package as registered mail, certified mail, insured, or collect on delivery (COD).

If you opened the package, then determined it was damaged, call the company and let them know it was received in damaged condition; in some cases, they will want you to give them a "return authorization number." Then send it back according to their instructions, along with a short note.

Sample Letter

1 March 1988

Mrs. Jackie Jackson
2032 Main Street
Hampton, VA 24040

Living Dolls, Inc.
Attn: Mrs. Janet Jones,
Manager, Customer Service
2040 Lindall Lane
Waukegan, IL 40402

Dear Ms. Jones,

I spoke with you on the phone today about Collector's Doll #1, which arrived by parcel post in damaged condition.

You indicated that upon receipt of the damaged doll, you would ship me a replacement.

I am enclosing the Collector's Doll #1, which I ordered on February 2, 1988, for which I paid $35.00 by personal check, number 403.

Sincerely,

Mrs. Jackie Jackson

4. *Sexually-Oriented Mail.* If you get unsolicited sexually-oriented mail, contact your local Postmaster, who will give you a standard form that will be sent to the sender. (Keep in mind that once you get on one mailing list, you'll get on others, too. It may take a while to get off these lists.)

5. *Unordered merchandise.* If you receive a product by mail that you did not order, which arrived through the U.S. mail, it's yours to keep; the sender cannot pressure you to pay for it or return it.

Be *sure* it's unordered merchandise by checking other members of the family to make sure they didn't order it, either.

6. *Late delivery.* The Federal Trade Commission requires that a mail order company must adhere to the following guidelines:

—They must ship you the product when they said they would.

—If no time was stated, they must ship the product within 30 days after they received your order with payment.

—If you used a credit card or charge card, the 30 days begin when you are *charged.*

If there is a delay, the mail order company must notify you when the product will be shipped. If it is more than 30 days after the promised date, then you can cancel the order and get a complete refund, or accept the new date; in either case, you must do so in writing.

Once you notify the mail order company that you want to cancel, the company has seven working days after receiving the cancelled order to give you a complete refund, if you paid by money order or check; if you used a charge card or credit card, the merchant has one billing cycle to credit your account.

There are exceptions to the FTC Mail Order Rule; write to the FTC for a current list of exceptions.

Key Addresses

To remove your name from mailing lists:
Direct Marketing Association
Attn: Mail Preference Service
6 East 43rd St.
New York, NY 10017

To contact the FTC:

Consumer Inquiries
Federal Trade Commission
Washington, DC 10580

If you suspect mail fraud:
Contact your local Postmaster, local Postal Inspector, or the Chief Postal Inspector:

Chief Postal Inspector
U.S. Postal Service
Room 3517
Washington, DC 20260-2100

Chapter **8**

Recommended Resources

Information is power, but only if you know where to look. Access to information is a problem; there are many books, magazines, reference books, and pamphlets of varying quality in print.

Here's what I recommend and why:

Books

1. *Consumer's Directory* (96 pp., $3.50), available by mail from: Everybody's Money, P.O. Box 431, Madison, WI 53701. A complete listing of product manufacturers grouped by industry or product, this directory provides with each listing the complete mailing address, phone number, and the name of its chief executive officer or president. In addition, the directory lists government and consumer agencies: federal agencies, FTC (Federal Trade Commission) regional offices, state and local government agencies, consumer leagues and organizations, U.S. senators and representatives, and federal information centers where you can get information about the federal government or secure help for a specific problem. The purpose of the centers is to give you an answer or put you in touch with someone who has the answer. An alphabetical index makes this resource easy to use.

2. *Consumer's Resource Handbook* (91 pp., free), available from *Handbook,* Consumer Information Center, Pueblo, CO 81009. This reference book has a very detailed listing of sources for consumer assistance that includes:

Corporate consumer contacts
Automobile manufacturers corporate contacts
Better Business Bureaus (U.S. and Canadian)
Industry third-party dispute resolution programs
Trade associations
State, county and city government consumer protection offices
State banking authorities
State commissions and offices on aging
State utility commissions
State weights and measures offices
Selected federal agencies
Military commissary and exchange contacts
Federal information centers
Services for handicapped persons
State vocational and rehabilitation agencies

A detailed index makes this reference book easy to use.

3. *Getting More for Your Money* (383 pp., $8.95), by the Better Business Bureau, published by Grosset and Dunlap. A collection of the

Bureau's pamphlets covering diverse subjects of consumer interest, this book was revised in 1983. Benjamin Company did a separate edition, available by mail. Currently, both editions are out-of-print. Check your library if you want to read a copy. (Alternately, the Better Business Bureau will send you a list of brochures available for a self-addressed-stamped envelope. Write to the Bureau at 845 Third Avenue, New York, NY 10022.)

4. *Everybody's Guide to Small Claims Court* (264 pp., $6.95) by Ralph Warner. A Nolo Press book, published by Addison-Wesley Publishing Company, the author is an attorney who takes you on a step-by-step process on everything you'd need to know about the small claims court process.

5. *How to Avoid Lawyers* (no pagination; 500 pages of clear text, 700 pages of forms, $22.95) by Don Biggs, with the help of two legal consultants. A massive book, subtitled "a step-by-step guide to being your own lawyer in almost every situation," this book is, according to its author, "a book of legal action. It does more than merely hand you an instruction manual with a bit of information with which to defend yourself within the legal jungle. It gives you the weapons you need to take the initiative in dealing with landlords and merchants, insurance companies and home improvement contractors, attorneys and creditors, and courts and the federal government."

6. *You Can Negotiate Anything* (255 pp., Lyle Stuart, Inc.) by Herb Cohen. The most readable and useful book on negotiation, Cohen shows how you are a negotiator even if you don't think so, then goes on to show how you can take control of a situation.

Magazines

1. *Changing Times,* published by The Kiplinger Magazine, is a monthly publication available by subscription or at the bookstore or newsstand. This magazine, like other consumer magazines, takes the position that you the buyer should know *before* you buy. Articles cover how to buy new products and services, weighing pros and cons, but not rating each product in comparative fashion like *Consumers Union.*

2. *Consumers Digest,* published by Consumers Digest, Inc. Published once every two months, this general interest consumer magazine is available at bookstores, newsstands, or by subscription for $15.95 a year.

3. *Consumer Reports,* published by Consumers Union, a not-for-profit organization. This magazine is a monthly, available at bookstores, newsstands, or by subscription. An unbiased evaluater that tests and evaluates diverse products, *Consumer Reports* does not accept advertising.

About the Author

A firm believer in complaining to companies when things go wrong, Mr. Beahm has written many complaint letters to large and small companies alike, locally and nationally.

Writing to virtually every kind of product manufacturer and service industry, Mr. Beahm assumes that everything is negotiable and uses complaint letters to voice his opinion to get what he feels he's paid for.

With files of successful letters of complaint as proof, Mr. Beahm firmly believes that you *must* complain when things go wrong because if you don't, who will?

Other books by the author:
How to Buy a Woodstove and Not Get Burned!
How to Sell Woodstoves
How to Publish and Sell Your Cookbook
Kirk's Works
The Vaughn Bode Index

ORDER FORM

NOTE TO THE READER

Please patronize your local bookstore, but if you can't find this book there, you can order direct from The Donning Company by using the order form below.

Please send check or money order to:

The Donning Company/Publishers
Attn: Direct Mail Dept.
5659 Virginia Beach Boulevard
Norfolk, VA 23502

Please allow 4 weeks for shipping.

QUANTITY	TITLE	PRICE	TOTAL
	Write To The Top	$5.95 each	
	Shipping		$2.00
	VA residents only add $.27 sales tax per book		
		TOTAL	

Name _____

Address _____

City _____ State _____ Zip _____

Index